My Sound of Song

Karmen Worden

ISBN 978-1-64028-498-2 (Paperback)
ISBN 978-1-64028-499-9 (Digital)

Copyright © 2017 by Karmen Worden
All rights reserved. No part of this publication may be reproduced, distributed, or transmitted in any form or by any means, including photocopying, recording, or other electronic or mechanical methods without the prior written permission of the publisher. For permission requests, solicit the publisher via the address below.

Christian Faith Publishing, Inc.
296 Chestnut Street
Meadville, PA 16335
www.christianfaithpublishing.com

Printed in the United States of America

Poetry

A Cinderella Story 6
The Spirit's Call 14
The Cries of Creation 21
The Gift of the Spirit 27
The Foggy Terrain 30
Song of the Wind 40
The North Window 50
My Hear Has to Know 53
Was This the Plan? 71
Called The Rhythm of Life 72
The Heavenly Song 83
Darkness in the Valley 94
Numb from the Predator's Blow 96
The Seashell 97
The Dance 99
Identity Crisis 100
The Ripple 102
A Message to My Deceased Husband 103
Confusion 104
My Play 105
Fear of Storms 107
Blown with the Wind 109
The Awakening 110
My Tree 111
The Drama in the Flower Bed 119

For the Love of Lyrics 121
I Wondered 123
Heaven..123
Ella...131
Change of Pace...154
The Second Time Around 155

A Humble Beginning

As my new Israeli husband and I were traveling to my home town in Iowa for a wedding, I knew he would suffer a culture shock when we reached the farm where I grew up. He had never seen a farm in the United States. He was born in Israel and lived there during his grade school years during World War II when Israel was surrounded by war. We had been married just a few months when we left our beautiful home in a suburb of Washington, DC, for a wedding near my own home in Jackson, Iowa. This man had served in the Israeli Army before he came to go to a university in New York. Now he is a professional engineer working in the city and living in the suburbs. In the Middle West, he couldn't believe that while driving miles and miles, one could see only corn and bean fields.

With a bird's eye view in my earlier life, you would look down on our farm laid out in colorful patchwork squares like the country quilts that Mother and Grandma made for all the children and grandchildren. In one field of green, black and white Holstein cows grazed in a pasture of clover. The soybeans added another shade of green and the oats were like knee-high golden grass when the crop was ripe. That picture of harmony existed while I grew up on the farm as farmers had their own composition: which field needed to be used for different crops, the kind of fertilizer and seeds that would be planted depending on the winter moisture, and the timing of preparing the ground for planting. Timing comes with any discipline like in music or completing a list for going to town.

A Cinderella Story

With a different setting,
a country farm where we see her
walking to the well for water.
She carries a pail,
avoiding chicken droppings on the ground
on her way to the pump,
a necessary household job each day.
She passes an outhouse,
and near the barn she reaches the well
To pump and fill the
pail with water.

She didn't meet the world there.
It was still outside her radar,
entrenched, as she was,
in the daily life she lives.
Her insecurities ever firmly in place
near her home near where her Grandma
lives. Her favorite grandma who loves her.

Home on the flat country farm
with no hills in sight,
the beginning of early life
with its traditions and
narrow road we followed.
But it was the only life you can know
where you grow up with others like you.
Where was the world?

Back to the car to where City Man, who knew opera, classical music, and could sing the next line of either song is. Why would he choose an original country girl like me, who is now teaching in Virginia? This next fact adds intrigue to Christian readers. In high school, I was a fundamentalist believer in Christianity, while he was Jewish. You need to read my story to know why I would marry him, and why he would marry me! Could this composition make for a happy marriage?

In high school, I met my first husband. He came from another farm in the German part of the country, who also planned to go to the university and find a job somewhere else. I only dreamed of getting away. It would never occur to me while living in Iowa to marry outside of my faith. My sister and I shared a bedroom with a window where I could see the stars at night. Every night, I looked out of our upstairs bedroom window and say, "Star light, star bright, first star I see tonight. I wish I may, I wish I might, have the wish I wish tonight." I dreamed of leaving the farm.

The stars looked down from colorful place, but no one had time to look at the beauty. The days were full of work on our country farm, but Mother had become the family's weather watcher. "I don't like the looks of the sky," Mother would say one evening as she walked down the lane at the day's end while looking at the clouds in the western sky. Mother recognized when the clouds looked threatening and a storm might be coming our way. She understood the feeling in the air when the danger of a tornado was eminent. Sometimes in the middle of the night, Mother would wake us up, saying, "Quick! Kids, grab your shoes. We're going to the basement." And we would stay in the cold, often damp, basement just below the kitchen until the thunder was off in the distance and Mother felt it safe for us to go back to bed. A tornado could strip a farm with only the crops or just the home.

Then, my wish was always a prayer as I was close to God all of my life. I wished to find someone and get away from this awful farm that was smelly and dirty, and I hated chickens and wouldn't clean them. I had no idea what "getting away" meant. I had never been to a city. Mother would have been hysterical if I had chosen a Catholic, but we didn't have any of those in our town either. While I was growing up we were poor. We were landlocked from any water around except for the water in the gravel pit close to the town, but you had to be fearless to jump into that deep water-logged cavern. We didn't learn to swim.

I thought the stork had dropped me into the wrong family. I didn't believe in a stork. That was part of the joke of getting away. God knew I needed my first marriage to get away from the country, as well as to marry a Christian man who would be the father of my children. He was a loving, Christian husband.

Only God knew I would lose him young in life, and this Jewish man would be the next startling love for the second half of my life. How we got together is a strange but beautiful story. It's like a Cinderella story. Then later, a writer friend gave me the plan that I followed. After Eddie died, she said to pray about it and wait for the open door. That I did, and went on with my life after grief and met other men to date. After being with country husband, Eddie my whole life, I knew nothing of a city or people from the world outside of the Middle West.

Young country girl who liked to be barefoot outside, climb trees, and make bow and arrow from pieces of wood meets handsome businessman from Israel, who had been a child in Israel during World War II when fighting battered and pummeled around them. Then, Farm Child, Susanne, was a young child. He said that during the war, Israel was for R and R, which means soldiers from other countries fighting nearby could come to Israel for a rest and for good food on the beach. I asked Michael if he ever went down to the beach when soldiers were there. He said he and his friends did go to the beach, as the soldiers would throw them coins.

I didn't know then about his knowledge of books in the past, of authors, and of classical musical where he could sing the next phrase. Besides, he knew opera, and I repeat, he could sing the phrase following an aria. I didn't know I'd be marrying an encyclopedia. It was hidden, like finding a treasure that would to be explored. I learned this information about him as we sat around a table for our meals and afternoon coffee. Then, I'd go to my computer and continue writing a journal that tells the stories he told me about growing up in Israel. This would later be another book, for I was a writer throughout my teaching and into my retirement.

I have to stop the story to tell you how I knew the Jewish man was the right person for me. I was a facilitator of the support for widowed people for several years after my husband died young. A new man appeared one evening. He didn't seem to be the support group type, but I waited to see more of him. The last potluck of the Widowed Person Service, I saw him sitting in a corner with an ottoman in front of him. He didn't mix at all, and I stopped by to talk to him. We wore name tags, and my name (different from Susanne) had an unusual spelling. He said he remembered it when the announcement for the support group came again and my name was there. I had led the group for five years. This man seemed to be going everywhere I went without my giving him any encouragement.

After being single for several years and dating a number of men in the group, Jewish man asked me twice to accompany him to the Kennedy Center. I called my sister who was always my counselor. I said, "You know, I prayed about it and my friend said, 'Wait for the open door.' Now what do I do? This Jewish man has asked me again. He came from work wearing a suit. He is persistent, coming again, like he's coming to see me. He's such a nice man, but I don't want to lead him on. Would God really choose this man for me?"

My sister reminded me to "Wait for the open door," as my writer friend had said. So, I went to the Kennedy Center twice and then he asked me again. This wasn't a good move. He took me to see his home and he came by my house to talk. This was when he talked like we were a pair. He had chosen me, but no words to that effect came about except when he talked about what I could possibly get when he dies after I married him. I didn't take that seriously. Except, he wouldn't be saying that if he had not made up his mind about marrying me. You can see that the only reason I went with him was because I thought this was the open door.

I continued as if this must be the open door. Would God put a Jewish man in my sights? I continued going with him as if we would be a married couple. This man would never believe that praying to God would decide the right person to marry.

Then, when his sister and her husband from Israel came to visit us, they wanted to read my story. I heard laughing. I knew they were laughing about my feelings that I believed that God worked his way in my life. I think that they laughed because he had not been following me around. He had been following my breasts. Each man knows what he likes best about a woman, and this man loved breasts. At the first potluck dinner he attended, I wore a red sweater, and large breasts to me weren't a positive thing. How would he like to carry these heavy things around each day?

When Grief Had Passed

When grief had passed/ And I was alone/ Just over the hill/ I could not see/ The future that lay Ahead for me./ A dream, like an adventure/ An unknown frontier/ I did not know A loved one was near./ One night we met/ In a sharing group/ Where I visited briefly/ With someone new./ I did not know/ I left behind/ A glimpse of myself/ For I was blind/And paid no heed/ As I passed on by./

He knew at that moment/ Without reflecting/ That our colors were blending,/ A beauty foretelling./ Like a flicker of flame/ Igniting the way/ Spirit and heart/ Connecting one day./

How can one know/ What makes it right?/ Only God can know/ My friend had said,/ "Wait for a path/ That lies ahead/ With no branches covering/ The hidden divide,/ Then you'll be free/ To step inside."/

I believed it was true/ What my friend said before/ I never questioned/ The open door./ A memory lives on/ Alive in my brain/ and I hear it over/ and over again./ Like a beautiful

Song/ that brings on the tears,/ I'll remember his words/ Through the passing of years./

"Nothing will ever/ Keep us apart,/ For I have taken you/ Into my heart."/ No other words/ need Ever be heard/ That compares with Those beautiful/ Most tender of words.

That night, the third time to the Kennedy Center when he knew I was the one he wanted to marry, we came by my house and talked by the fireplace. Then, I gave him only the love he needed: my breasts. He was a man who loved breasts. I took off my blouse, and later I heard what he had told his friends. He thought he had died and gone to heaven when his face nestled into my large breasts.

Yes, when I called home saying I was going to get married, my sister gave me a lecture that could have come from my mother, who had been gone for many years. I called my daughter, and she gave me another lecture. I don't believe that at all. One son kept saying, "I can't believe it." The second son, who was married and wanted to keep his promise to his Japanese wife that he would spend some years working in Tokyo, was happy that he could now make new plans. None of my children had heard of this man. Wasn't that possible as this happened on the third date? And now you know how I thought this came about.

I will tell you later what my mother would have said about my second love. You need to know my story before you learn about this beautiful Jewish man who married a girl who used to be country, but who, during that time was a fundamentalist believing in the exact words of the Bible. Yet God had other plans before this part of the story could be told. Now, we are driving down the road to see the farm where I grew up.

As we drove into the lane, the farm buildings now aged and in their worst condition with paint weathered, doors sagging, and parts of the roof of the house caved in. I said, "Now you'll know, Michael, where your wife grew up. This is country in its worst condition. We didn't have an indoor bathroom. We had to bring in water from the pump." I pointed to the distance from the house, "We carried the dirty water to the closest fence with corn and dumped it in the field. This was hard work. I don't want to tell you this." I pointed to the space where the outhouse used to be parked. It was also a good place for a catalog that we never used. I never liked having a dress from feed sack materials. It was okay for country school, but *never* in high school. The country schools in Iowa closed, and I went to sixth grade in town school.

In the house, we had no indoor plumbing, no electricity, no bathroom, and no running water. As a young child, I remember an ice box for a few years before the REA (Rural Electric Association) brought electricity to the country. It was no easy task bringing electricity to the wide open spaces of the Middle West. In the winter, Dad used a lantern in the barn to milk the cows, and we used candles in the house at night when it got dark. During the daylight hours, Mom canned fruits and vegetables using a cook stove in the kitchen that burned dried-out corn cobs. But it helped to know that Michael knew about an ice box. They had one, too, during the early years.

The Spirit's Call

Time was when each of us all were new.
We were born all wrinkly and fair,
And that was the time when the Lord said goodby,
As He kissed us and put us here.

"Now, do the best that you can," he said.
"For life is not easy out there."
And then with a wave of His powerful hand,
"I'll be ever as close as a prayer."

As time went by, we blossomed and grew,
If we had enough nurturing and care.
But there was pain, along with the gain,
And it was hard to feel God was out there.

One day in my life when covered with rust,
The scars, the unfulfilling of dreams,
The Lord had His say in His most loving way,
"Child, life is more than it seems."

I've been waiting and wondering
These long years through
For you to view life through my sight,
And now that you've heard the Spirit's call
You will sleep and find peace in the night."

Time is when each of us all were old
When we were all wrinkly, yet fair,
This is the time when we say goodbye,
And He welcomes us into His care.

We never thought about being old at this time, but I'll leave that verse in. I remember sobbing at my Norwegian great-grandma's funeral. Her body was brought in the house. I've been emotional at every single funeral, so that verse stays because this is my story.

Now, we are back on the farm with my new husband. "The only farm I ever saw was on television," Michael said. "I watched the TV program called Bonanza, and on that show, the ranch, called the Ponderosa had a beautiful mansion with porches around most of the house—surrounded by green grasses and horses grazing in the fields."

First, I laughed. Then, I was shocked! If he had only seen the Ponderosa and he was facing my farmstead, we're comparing the workers' quarters to grounds of a palace. I said that I would never in the whole wide world *ever* be a farmer's wife. And in those younger years, would I think of marrying a Jew? Never! Jews lived in the Holy Land. But now I was with an intelligent, handsome Jewish man who came to see this farm.

Life in the Country

We helped with farm jobs such as carrying water from the pump at the other end of the yard that we would heat for washing dishes, making coffee, and taking a bath. We took dirty water and garbage outside and threw it over the fence of the field nearest our house.

Our feed for the animals came in patterned feed sacks which became cloth for some of our clothes. If a skirt or dress were too short, Mom sewed a strip of a plain colored fabric on the bottom. In country school, I wore overalls like my dad. But in town school when I was in fifth grade, we wore clothes like the other farm kids. You don't stand out if other farm kids are dressed just like you.

My father grew corn, beans, and oats. The pasture was for the cows we milked, the pigs we raised, and the chickens we used for meat and eggs. I walked barefoot in the summer, avoiding stinky chicken droppings in the yard. We kids were scared of the "fighty rooster." This was our term for the mean rooster who would come running toward us with his head down ready to attack. He didn't have other roosters as competition for his harem of hens and had to vent his aggression on us.

One day when I was in the chicken house with my dad, we looked in the small storage room in the corner where Dad kept feed for the chickens. There sat one hen sitting on a nest of burned-out light bulbs. What other proof did we need that chickens were on the low-end of the scale when it comes to animal intelligence?

We also feared our two-ton bull, who opened the gate of the cow yard with his horns and got out where we kids played. Coming home from school, we'd run from tree to tree while peering out to see if the bull was loose in the yard. This wasn't an idle threat since someone in Mother's family had been gored by a bull on his own farm. We never forgot that awful story. I kept thinking, he may have been in the barnyard on his own home and someone never heard him crying in time. How horrible a death that would be!

Either Jenna or I had to walk to the pasture in the late afternoon to bring the cows back to the barn to be milked. We were scared to death because the bull was a part of the herd. We thought he'd get mad if he sees a red color. Jenna once had to run for her life even when not wearing red. This is how we got the cows back to the barn: we opened the gate, walked toward the cows, and tried to move them toward the lane. The cows needed to come because their bags were full of milk, and that was my dad's job—to milk the cows. When the bull saw us, he lowered his head and bolted toward us like we were a threat to his personal space. Several times, we'd sprint with lightning speed to climb the fence before the bull reached us.

One game we liked to play was to walk the fence between the hog yard and the cow yard. The point of the game was to stay on the fence and not fall into something unpleasant on either side. Once, we tried to pass each other while we were going different directions, but that idea was futile. We didn't have toys, but Jenna and I shared one bicycle and our brother had one. Yet children today don't realize that you can have fun without toys that are purchased. It just takes creative minds. I learned by reading, raised my own children, and taught children that all of us have that gift of using our creative minds.

Dad raised hogs. The sow (the mother hog) could have as many as ten piglets at a time. Sometimes, the small one (a runt) could not get to the nipples for milk. Then, the piglet couldn't fight for itself and would remain small without our intervention. We would take the piglet in a box and into the porch, or into the house behind the cook stove in the kitchen if it was too cold outside. We would feed the piglet from a bottle until it was big enough to fight for itself. Then, we put him back with the mother and her other piglets.

In the very early years, Dad used two work horses, Bud and Bill, to pull the wagon filled with manure to fertilize the farm crops. For most of our childhood, he used a tractor with the other farm implements, and we could sometimes ride on the metal piece over the huge wheels. In the winter when we three kids wanted to sled, Dad pulled our sleds with the tractor because there were no hills for miles around.

Mother kept our house as clean as she could. She boiled white clothes in a large metal cooker on the kitchen stove. Even in the winter, we hung clothes out on the line and brought them into the house dry but frozen solid. We used newspapers to line our cupboards and the floor because farmers' shoes aren't clean. We used catalogs in the two-hole outhouse during the seasons when we could go outdoors. Life was hard work in the country before electricity came to the countryside.

One other bit of information you need to know was that Mother didn't give me the kind of love that I needed. I'll say it this way. I didn't know it then, but Mother didn't love me. I was too hyperactive, and she was either too tired or was too tired of me. She lost Alvin, her baby before me, and she got pregnant right away. She was exhausted and was still grieving and in pain. I admit that the great-grandma, whom I loved, was Dad's mother, and she was like a workhorse. She kept Mom moving. For example, when they were cleaning chickens and had already cleaned ten, Mom wanted to quit, but Grandma would say, "But we only have ten more to do. Let's finish them up." And Mother always gave in to Grandma. Also, we were a very religious family. I loved the Lord from the beginning of my time. I also treasured my grandma.

We bought necessary items such as flour and sugar in our little town of a thousand people. Money was scarce, but my parents never hesitated about piano lessons and buying a saxophone in high school band. But I knew they gave to us children rather than buy for their own needs, like leaving dental work until they needed false teeth.

They borrowed money from the bank to pay for one year of college for each of us three children which we paid back after we found a job. I never knew until later, the sacrifices they made to give us this luxury of a college education that they never had. All three of us siblings graduated from college with degrees in education for my sister and me, and engineering for my brother.

College prepared me for a world outside of our early beginnings. But nothing compared to the education I would experience later when I married my husband who was from a neighboring farm and from my high school. This brings up the matter of where people settled when they moved to the country. During the earliest times, the Swedes, Norwegians, and Germans usually moved down to Iowa from Minnesota or Wisconsin as they often came from the St. Lawrence River through one Great Lake after another until they came to Wisconsin or Illinois. Originally, they wrote back to their relatives in Europe that work was plentiful here, and that's how others came to the Middle West.

Often, they could get jobs with lumbering for building houses and farm buildings. And when settlers came to Iowa, they could get land at a very low price. In our town, Norwegians, Swedes, and Germans built their houses, a church, and a cemetery in clusters to be by their own people who still spoke their foreign languages. That's what happened in Iowa. Some of the Germans settled east of town where my husband's family lived.

They farmed on that land close to their church and cemetery where my husband was later buried. Others settled near my family's land to the southern part of the township. They built a country school where my dad went to school, and later my sister, brother, and I walked a half mile there. When the Norwegian community built a new church in town, that's where my German husband and I were married. This is how the early people settled on the land near their own people who originally used their foreign language.

I met my husband in high school and we planned to marry when both of us finished college. However, Iowa had a two-year degree for teaching elementary school. I completed my education in Luther College and was able to get a teaching job close to Iowa State University where my husband Eddie worked on his degree in agriculture. Later, after he graduated and both of us taught school, Eddie knew he could not make progress without getting a PhD. That's how we ended up later in Pammel Court, the metal housing for graduate students for $29.00 a month. Those tin huts, which we called them, were comfortable enough for early years of marriage.

There were years of teaching for both of us—banking for Eddie—while I taught sixth grade until we moved to Washington, DC. Then, we told our families goodbye and everyone was crying as we drove away to the suburbs of Washington, DC, with our three children ages two, four, and seven. I didn't have any reservations about Eddie's ability to handle anything he was expected to do. He would love this setting near Washington, DC, and his degree in economics kept us there until he died in 1993.

How can a smile,
a slight expression,
a tear, a sigh,
a quick confession,
a movement of hand,
the wave of an arm,
suddenly stimulate,
arouse, or alarm,
causing something to pass
through the atoms of space,
enter the mass of another's face
and instigate fear
or precipitate peace
or instill a sense
of a sudden release,
a chemical flow
of venom
or glow!

The Cries of Creation

If the earth were created just as it says
In the first book of the Bible, in Genesis,
We can imagine the earth-with some
Ear-splitting nights. For certain—man
Cries hearing, bone-chilling fights.

The earth came alive with living things,
Beasts of prey, and birds with wings,
Rodents, reptiles, and fish in the seas,
And a multitude of creatures that
Lived in the trees.

Sometimes, they were rowdy, a chorus of cries,
And ear-splitting screams, and snarls and sighs.
The sounds were cooing, and cawing, and croaking,
And howls tweeting and twittering, and
Screeching of owls.

Some animals roared. Some yelped in the dark.
Others gave a small cackle, a grunt, or a bark.
Some sounds were deafening. Some clear and sweet,
But the concert had melody, rhythm, and beat.

This was creation, new life on the land
And the creatures that played in the animal band,
And the sun went down on another night.
There was more to come when the day turned light.

The humans were created the following day,
And missed the symphony, the first creatures play.
They had their own problems to contemplate.
"Let's go back," they said, "to the Garden's gate.

"Maybe God will let us start over again
To change the outcome of this terrible sin."
But the cries that rang out much later that night
Weren't just for the animals that gave them fright.

As their voices cried out a mournful refrain,
Only God could hear their anguishing pain.

Creation of Mothers

God didn't write the story of creation, but the effects of this story have caused serious complications. These are my thoughts, one at a time, and I'm sharing my belief that the stories define God's nature as promoting man sovereign by creating him first. Of all of the problems, this was the worst.

No equality for women since the beginning of earth, and it's resulting with women as having less worth in the eyes of society, as man used his power to dominate and manipulate as we trembled and cowered in humiliation and degradation from generation to generation.

Each precious life who has lived on this earth, came about through a mother who gave that soul birth. We, Eves of the world, have been given such power to nurture each life every hour by hour. Then, how could one think we're inferior to man, when the honor was given by God's loving hand?

It fills me with sadness to know that a prayer is repeated each morning by a group who would dare to deny that God gave their women this power as they say every day in the early morning hour, "Thank you, God, that I was not created woman." Yes, we women have been blessed every day in this life, and this honor was given not to husband but his wife. (Orthodox Jews pray this each morning when they get up.)

Moving on in this story, if it is no fib, every man on this earth should be missing one rib. Early men who were doctors needed to know, so they dug up old corpses to see if it was so. They truly thought that the story of Eve was a fact that they could truly believe. You can see that this story has caused so much friction that some intelligent beings consider it fiction.

The second problem came from the warning that was given about the Tree of Knowledge somewhere in Eden, probably in the center with temptation ensuing, while Satan was watching and trouble was brewing. Didn't the writer of Genesis know that God knew before it had happened what they would go through? And the result of their sin, too excessive to trust, was that the punishment would continue to present day—*for us.*

Now, we toil the soil and it provides for our needs. We care for the animals, plants, grass, and seeds. God asked us to care for this planet in the future, our polluted earth, now a hard place to nurture. For all of this time, our load is too great, while we live out each day in a "fallen state." Sin follows us around everywhere that we go like a shadow it tails us. There's no escaping, we know.

Some Christian folks think they can't question one word in the story of Genesis, or they'll be referred to as lacking in faith and irreverent, too. They'll end up in hell, this being their due. Now we know a new story—the scientists' voices. We are here on this earth with far different choices.

Scientists say we evolved through mutations of genes that progressed through millions of years, so it seems. The Human Spark was ignited—the brain growth rampaging. To this day human growth adds new knowledge of aging.

Some may be incensed that I write this at all. "You cannot question Genesis or not believe the fall." Yes in Genesis, we know the Adam and Eve way when the earth was created in one week, day by day.

But if man came about through mutations of genes, it's God's plan I am sure, whatever the means.

New Beginning in the Suburbs

When my husband graduated from Iowa State University in Ames, Iowa, with a PhD, we, with our three children, moved to a suburb of Washington, DC, in Virginia. We experienced many changes such as an "open school system" where several grades could be taught in the same classroom with each child learning at his own individual pace. How different from my early years of teaching!

The Sermon

The experience that affected me the most, happened during a sermon in the new mission church we had joined. I had been programmed since birth to believe only in the inerrant Word of God, and hearing a different sermon caught me by surprise. This sermon seemed to challenge those beliefs and concentrate on the meaning of the passages. Suddenly, I was thrust into an exciting world of change that would continue to stimulate my interest in spirituality and what it meant to be a Christian.

The most important point about the sermon on Transfiguration was when Jesus took three of his disciples up on the mountain. They heard God's voice and the most literal interpretation of the Bible would say that Jesus' clothes turned absolutely white in one translation (gloriously white). Later I explained how this one sermon changed my life.

But we have to go back to a real important point theme in my story about living with depression. People need to know this, as I'd go through problems with people knowing it and then rejecting me. It's a disease you have to live with, yet you can't tell anyone. People need to know that with the proper medication you can live with depression. The story starts here.

The Gift of the Spirit

We marvel with awe at the raindrops,
Watch them disappear in the ground.
We know not what happens
When they leave our sight
Until life again blooms all around.

We ponder as we look at the snowflakes,
Watch the build-up of drifts on the ground.
How can You make each new pattern
With no flakes the same to be found?

We know You created the sounds of the birds.
You hear what they say in their song.
You miss the small voice of the sparrow
When it falls and the song is long gone.

We hear Your voice in the thunder.
We fear for the threatening storm.
And then when the danger is over,
A rainbow of promise is born.

We feel your breath in the breezes.
We hear your power in the wind.
But the greatest miracle of all, my Lord,
Is the gift of your Spirit within.

The first unsettling event happened in the Quonset hut housing where I was isolated in the winter with my daughter and two other children in my care. The Quonset huts were tiny bungalows with high windows covered with plastic to keep out the cold and to limit light in the rooms. One stove in the living room needed a fan fastened near the ceiling to blow heat back to the bedrooms. One night, I put a bowl of water under the bed in the winter (to prove a point) and it was frozen by morning. I couldn't go anywhere without a car, and Eddie could concentrate better in the university library.

I felt cut off from the world. It was difficult after four years of teaching school, which was a challenge I loved. Soon, I began to feel ill. My head was too heavy for my body and there was a lump in my throat. I saw a doctor who prescribed tranquilizers, but I was so tired from the side effects of the medication that I lay on the couch and could no longer care for the other two children. But I never neglected my precious daughter during those difficult weeks. I had waited five years for this child, and required a major surgical procedure before I could have children. She became the most essential focus of my life, *but what could be happening to me in my life?*

Finally, after two weeks on tranquilizers, the doctor prescribed an antidepressant and every symptom disappeared. I thought my depression was caused by the situation in my life: no friends, no time for myself, and caring for three small children in a tiny, cold house. I never considered that this was the beginning of periods of depression which later would be diagnosed as a chemical imbalance in my brain. I did not realize until later that I was predisposed to depression which had made life difficult for my mother and grandmother. As my story moves on, you will learn that depression struck all three of us in the family. My sister's son committed suicide when he was eighteen, and my brother's son disappeared in Chicago. They were frantic, and then he called home for his father to pick him up. This disease is that serious that my depression is caused by my brain lacking certain chemicals.

Thankfully, after the medication took effect, I felt such a release from this first experience of dark days. After two months, I didn't need antidepressants for several years. I know now that our brains need certain chemicals to function properly, and for those of us who have depression, doctors sometimes need to experiment to find the right medication for each individual. The drug the doctor gave me is used even today years later, and a search of the Internet tells me that researchers do not know exactly why it works. However, it was a miracle drug for me and I will be on this medication, with others added, for the rest of my life.

Surprisingly, depression didn't appear as sadness. It felt like a sickness with physical symptoms that could have been caused by any number of different problems. Awareness of the different symptoms for depression would be crucial later in life, when depression would emerge again causing unbelievable heartaches, not only for me but also in the families of my sister and my brother. We knew it was a chemical imbalance in my brain and medication was necessary to live a normal life. It was a new life after the depression was gone.

It is so important for me to be a spokesperson to shout out to the world that depression is an illness no more different than a diabetic needing insulin. But we know it is different in the perception people have. People can turn against you, as they did for me when I shared it with a discussion group. We were discussing a book with the character having depression. I thought it was a perfect time to share this fact as I am a living example that I could live a normal life and can even teach in school.

The Foggy Terrain

When you have entered the foggy terrain,
You and the real you are not the same.
The lens through which you see is not reality.
The real you with hopes and dreams,
Visions, yearnings, and what could be
Now—no possibility.

Like insulin needed for another condition
But with depression, you have a different rendition.
You cannot tell others. They cannot know,
With an illness like this that doesn't show.
I heard someone say, "She takes that pill,
The one for someone who is mentally ill."
Then when it's known, you are left all alone.

Neurotransmitters need a chemical change,
With the right medications, the doctors explain.
Only then will you leave the foggy terrain
When you and real you are exactly the same.
Then you'll experience the joy you share
When you do the things for which you care.

Enlightenment in Liberal Leanings

I came to Virginia still a fundamentalist believing in the literal interpretation of the Bible. The sermon on the Transfiguration explained that Jesus had taken three of his disciples, Peter, James, and John, up a high mountain by themselves. Suddenly, a change came over Jesus, and they witnessed his clothes becoming shining white. They saw Jesus talking to Moses and Elijah on the mountain, and heard the voice of God saying, "This is my own dear Son. Listen to Him." The disciples were terrified. Peter wanted to build three tents in their honor. As they came down the mountain, Jesus told them not to tell anyone about the incident. I can imagine how scared they would be. This sermon hit me like lightning as well, and I have never forgotten it. Later, when Michael and I went to Israel, I asked to be taken up that mountain.

The pastor's emphasis in the sermon was not that the robe turned white, but that the disciples saw Jesus in a completely different light. The robe, although it could have turned white, didn't have to literally turn white. Paraphrasing my understanding of the story about Moses and Elijah: they saw Jesus as significant in their lives, as Moses and Elijah were significant to the Jewish people of Israel.

At the time, I was shocked. If we don't view the Transfiguration literally, this leaves the door open to discuss the meaning of any story in the Bible. I was ready for new change from my mother's way of thinking. The creation story of Adam and Eve tells us that God created this world and it was good. Without the literal interpretation, Christians can accept the scientific view that our earth is millions of years old and that the human spirit could have entered the world in a much different way. Wow!

Prediction of a Fiery Future

I continued to attend Bible studies, to read books, and to take classes at the university to prepare for teaching school again. My biggest mistake was sharing one insignificant thought with my mother, and that was saying I wasn't sure that angels existed. She didn't say anything to me, but she took it to heart and told family members that I had taken the wrong road. I was on my way to hell. I wish I could think about it without it making me angry all over again. I thought that counseling helped me recover from lack of a mother's love. I had recovered, but God knows the pain just can't be eliminated as if it were an insect you can step on.

I didn't pay any attention to Mother's forecast for my future, but my subconscious mind was quite awake and was filing the experience with other ideas that provided a connection that caused a small growth to begin swelling in my subconscious mind. The infection would later affect every cell in my body.

Years later after my husband died and I married a Jewish man who had grown up in the holy land of Israel, I felt it necessary to look at Christianity from an outsider's perspective. I wondered if my views of Christianity would change as I associated with people who did not believe in Jesus! I wondered if Israel would continue to be a "holy land" to me when we visited my husband's family in

Israel with all of them in the secular beliefs of Judaism. In addition, I always had to answer to people who knew me, "How could a good Christian like you, Susanne, marry a Jew?" Thankfully, our roads take us only small steps at a time without ever knowing where that path will lead us and surprising even ourselves. But we aren't there in this story. I'm living with the man whom I love, as we raised three beautiful children under the influence of a Protestant Church.

Surprisingly, depression didn't appear as sadness. It felt like sickness: physical symptoms that could have been caused by any number of different problems. Awareness of the different symptoms for depression would be crucial later in life, when depression would emerge again causing unbelievable heartaches, not only for me but also in the families of my other two siblings.

This awareness of my love for change and the unconventional would prepare me for the significant differences in my life after our move to the suburbs of a city. I was someone who became excited about new experiences. I didn't know how much I would metamorphose into a different person later in my life. Much later, "unconventional" became a norm for me, surprising my family and everyone else who had ever known me.

But love for change didn't fit with my mother. Her beliefs were rigid and I did not confront her while at home. I still believed in the fundamentalist views of the church. Not until we moved and found a new home in VA and a new modern Lutheran Church did I hear the exciting sermon that changed me. This was the sermon on the Transfiguration of Jesus on the mountain when Jesus went there with his three loving disciples. I have been on the top of the mountain. I know it's not the mountain or any location that causes changes, but the connection to Jesus as I know him now really—began in a sermon about Jesus on the top of that mountain. Remember that this new husband was a Jewish man who was born in Tel Aviv, Israel, which I visited with him for six times.

Later in Israel, I asked Michael's sister to take me to the top of that mountain. She took me there, and from there, you are above the whole country of Israel. It was as beautiful a sight as it looks today, and I was happy to be in the same place where Jesus had been given this message from God.

Creation

God didn't write the story of creation, but the effects of this story have caused serious complications. These are my thoughts one at a time, sharing my belief that the stories define God's nature as promoting man sovereign, creating him first. All of the problems, this was the worst.

No equality for women since the beginning of earth, and it's resulting with women as having less worth in the eyes of society as man used his power to dominate, manipulate as we've trembled and cowered in humiliation and degradation from generation to generation.

Each precious life who's lived on this earth came through a mother who gave that Soul birth. We, Eves of the world, have been given such power to nurture each life every hour by hour. Then how could one think we're inferior to man, when the honor was given by God's loving hand.

It fills me with sadness to know that a prayer----is repeated each morning by a group who would dare to deny that God gave their women this power as they say every day in the early morning hour, "Thank you God, that I was not created woman." Yes, we women have been blessed every day in this life, and this honor was given, not to husband but his wife.

Moving on in this story if it is no fib, every man on this earth should be missing one rib. Early men who were doctors needed to know, so they dug up old corpses to see if it was so. They truly thought that the story of Eve was a fact that they could truly believe. You can see that this story has caused so much friction that some intelligent beings consider It fiction.

The second problem came from the warning that was given about the Tree of Knowledge somewhere in Eden, probably in the center—with temptation ensuing, while satan was watching and trouble was brewing. Didn't the writer of Genesis know that God knew before it had happened—what they would go through. And the result of their sin, too excessive to trust, that the punishment would continue to present day--FOR US.

Distressing Developments

Our future in Virginia seemed very bright to my husband and me. We both had good jobs, our daughter loved university life, and the boys were in their last years of high school when my husband's diabetes intensified from pills to daily doses of insulin. He hadn't been following his diet or checking his blood sugar, which resulted in sores on his feet that weren't healing. The doctor tried bed rest for a couple of weeks and even time in the hospital. But time came for when he had to use crutches to go to work.

Then one day, he developed an illness which seemed like a bacterial infection and the doctor prescribed antibiotics. Yet he became worse and was flown by helicopter to Richmond, Virginia, the only hospital in the area to do heart transplants. Tests showed that a virus had attacked his heart with fifty percent damage to the left ventricle. After three weeks in the hospital trying other forms of treatment, he was sent home with heart medications and frightening news.

"With the heart damage you have," the doctor said to Eddie. "You will have about three years to live!" We were numb with the possibility of his death. I couldn't believe this sudden change in our lives. How could something as simple and common as a virus, damage the heart to that extent? How could I finance college for my three children on my income from teaching school? After a few weeks with the help of the heart medications and a specialist watching his diabetes, he was able to return to work and life went on in the human race and in our family.

Our two sons joined rock bands under the direction of the music teacher at school. One of them was practicing drums in my basement, while the other was spending hours on his guitar learning new music and writing his own original pieces. My husband and I missed the Battle of the Bands, a popular contest in the high school with the rock-type band groups competing for first place. While I was in the Richmond Hospital with Eddie, we were happy to hear that our older son's rock group won first place that year.

Teaching became my escape and respite from thoughts of my husband's illness. Throughout my teaching career, I searched for creative ideas to help children experience a love of learning through topics in social studies and through novels in reading class. While studying about Greece, the students performed Greek plays. When we studied "early man," I wrote a thirty-minute musical called "The Cave Man Rap" given for the other fifth-grade classes during the day and for the parents in the evening. I had been working on a family history for several years and continued adding pictures and stories to my family's ancestral heritage.

But the thoughts that my husband and I would not be spending most of our future together changed my life, like looking through a lens of sadness. My husband lived for nine years, but several of those years were painful and traumatic as time passed and he knew his life was running out. How can one have this knowledge and live a normal life? But that was what we tried to do.

Song of the Wind

"From where did you come?"
I asked the soft breeze,
"And where do you go
when you're gone?"
"I come from far off,
from the Seven Seas.
Don't you hear the sound
of my song?

I sing as I move from
here to there.
I sing as I follow the bay.
And sometimes I cry
as I move on by
For the things
that I witness each day.

Sometimes, I am weak,
And I whisper a prayer.
Sometimes I am strong and bold.
Do you think I know
where I come and go?
Some power keeps me moving along.
I've been around
since time was new,
When the rhythm of life first began.
I have watched generations
as they've come along.
They've all heard the
sound of my song."

As life went on, I volunteered at school to learn the latest methods in education. I taught Sunday school and Bible School. In addition, I began classes at the university to finish my degree. My story explores the effects of depression, grief, and the process of recovery rather than telling the beautiful and rewarding side of my life and raising my children. But nothing in life can compare with the pleasure of raising my children. I watched them grow and change and saw the individual traits that are a part of each unique child. No joy compares to the mother's love I have for each of my children.

How Depression Progressed

During Eddie's illness, my doctor worked with me to stabilize my life and selected medications that would help me. These medications are different for everyone because of the different chemicals in our brains that cause depression. One chemical, serotonin, contributes to feelings of well-being plus other functions like regulating mood and helping with memory and learning. My doctor explained that my medication has two different chemicals and serotonin is one of them.

I think it's important for people with depression to go to a psychiatrist who has been trained in the use of these medications, as there's no test to determine which chemical works for an individual person. The doctor may need to try different types of medications, and watch for results which may take a few weeks to have an effect. If the patient feels no change in the depression, then another kind of medication can be substituted.

My doctor found a medication that worked for me for many years. Then, one time before my husband died, I said to my internist, "Why couldn't you prescribe my antidepressant instead of my seeing the psychiatrist every year?" He said he could certainly do that and prescribed Prozac, a popular drug. The reason I asked my doctor (of internal medicine) if he could prescribe medication for depression was because I came to my psychiatrist only for refills to my medication. Each visit, she did needlework while she sat in her chair. Yes, she asked how I was doing, and I said I was free from depression. She said, "As long as you take this kind of medication I prescribe, you have depression."

I felt wonderful on Prozac and thought I finally had gotten my life together. I didn't need as much sleep. I was so excited about the writing that when a new idea came to me in the night, I'd get up at 3:00 a.m. to work on the article before going back to bed. It was such a productive and electrifying time of my life for about a month—until I hit a low. I continued to teach school, but I knew I was in a deep depression. I cannot tell you how hard it was to function every day in school but I did. I seem to have another side of my life which I call my shadow. Like any shadow, it's with you forever. I considered it my duty to keep as normal a life as possible and to be a good teacher for my students. My personal self always came last. I can truthfully say that I had a self that could function well on the medication, and I thought I was a good teacher.

I had a shadow with everyone except my sister. I was like "Two Faces of Eve," one side would appear when I was with people. I had "Two Faces of Susanne" and only one side would appear when I was with people. This "Second Face of Suzanne" worked, or I would not have been able to continue my teaching career. Even my children did not know that I had the condition of depression.

They were all in college when this happened. I never shared my shadow with anyone except my counselor and my sister.

This was the only time in my teaching experience when a student didn't like me and let me know it constantly by his work and behavior. I wanted the administrator to take him out of my class, but principals don't like to move a child during the school year. Finally, the school counselor called a meeting for the parent, child, and me in her office. I've never walked out of a meeting in my life. But after it started, I knew I would suddenly cry if I didn't leave the room, so I just walked out! I had to live with that child in my class for the rest of the year. Somehow I survived, but those were the worst months in my teaching career.

I went back to my psychiatrist to explain my manic attacks about a month of highs followed by a month of lows. She immediately changed my prescription to the one that had previously worked effectively. It is a miracle drug for some people. But for me, it was a nightmare for several months. However, the cycles of highs and lows didn't disappear immediately when I started the new medication. I continued to cycle for several months, although each cycle was less severe than the one before.

The cycle of highs and lows gradually weakened, but Prozac had such a negative effect on my brain that the cycles had to gradually wear out before they disappeared forever. Don't let any doctor except a psychiatrist prescribe your medication for depression. They do not know all the new medications and how they interact. They have not had to keep abreast of that condition as there are too many different diseases that a specialist has to know. Although I liked and respected my doctor's ability to keep anew on other drugs, psychiatry is a dangerous condition that can cause someone to slip into the crack and commit suicide.

Suicide can be a consequence for undiagnosed and serious depression as I will explain in a later part of my story after Jenna's son "suicided." (Jenna said a verb is the correct use, rather than a noun like he committed suicide.) Now I know the pain that the family experiences after such a tragedy. I admit that, while I am in a depression, I wish I did not feel that life is not worth living. I don't want to think that I would prefer to be dead rather than alive. I fight this thought because I am so appreciative of all the beautiful pieces (like a slice of a pie) that I am so thankful for.

Then when guilt overwhelms me, the sunny side of my shadow tries to keep me from even thinking of causing my own death: guilt to God, to my beautiful life, to my wonderful husband, and to my children. A guilt so heavy that I cannot even mention it more. I will explain this later, as people need to have these facts about depression. But something else comes first: my vision of the devil. This serious problem with my mother added to my neurotransmitters that light up my brain when I need a medication changed.

In depression, my busy brain didn't work like it did before. I felt I had no talent to do anything. I wanted to stay home from groups that I joined, and it is hard to concentrate on a novel. Jenna, my sister with her counseling degree, has always been my only help. No one other than Jenna, who lost her beautiful child to suicide, knows what depression is all about. Talking to a psychiatrist would not have helped since these symptoms were caused by a chemical imbalance. Thankfully, I had a side of myself that could function in my work and in my writing. It didn't function well with my husband because he was suffering from his own inner and outer problems at home and at work.

The Vision of the Devil

The first indications that I had inner turmoil occurred when our children were in high school and I was finishing a degree in Elementary Education to prepare for teaching in the public schools. It all started with an anxiety attack, which felt like electric charged currents running through my body—filling me with fear. At one time, I thought I was inside my body looking out through the keyholes of my eyes. I had also neglected an important deadline for graduation in the spring, caused my professor to angrily help me graduate from the university on time. I was frightened.

I talked to the pastor who gave me the name of a psychologist, and I remember sobbing until I was exhausted through the first session with him. He understood my mixed-up life about my mother's feelings about me and said that it took seven years of psychotherapy for him to overcome the religious beliefs enforced on him as a child. Most importantly, he gave me the confidence that I could call him day or night when the fear attacks began.

Through counseling, I learned that I had submerged intense, angry feelings about my mother who had often spoken about how difficult I was to raise. She never had warm words for me. She never had warm arms to hold me with nor had she ever heard me crying at night before I went to sleep. When my sister asked why I was crying, I always said that I didn't know. But usually, I was thinking that Mother would die.

During our earlier years, Mother would lose control of herself in spells of tempestuous tears, while we children stood fearfully outside of her bedroom. We were frightened at what was happening to her. We know now that both my grandma and my mother had depression without proper medication to control the disease. My mother's mother, my Swedish grandma, had a series of nervous breakdowns when she was raising her children.

Then, Mother's story to everyone. "I never thought I'd ever get her raised," Mother would tell people about me. "She ate food left out for the dog. She climbed on the table and ate the tassels off the curtains. She slept with one eye always open, so we could never get anything done." It took weeks of sobbing sessions to work through these issues, as well as a Rorschach test (the ink blot test asking what the person sees in black blotches of different shapes), which brought out shocking results. One of the tests displayed the reality of what my mother's views of religion had done to my life.

However, after I had children, I learned how hard it would have been for my mother to carry a baby for nine months while living in her mother's home with a doctor that could not handle her kind of pregnancy, then only to see that beautiful baby named Alvin die. I can feel the heartache.

After the Rorschach test that asks you what you see in black blotches of different shapes, you will then hear about the judgment from the psychiatrist who interprets the test.

On one black blotch, which could have a sexual interpretation, I said, "It looks like a vagina, but there are sharp pieces on the edges." He said I wanted to castrate men. How outrageous could that be? Could I trust any result from the test than could cause that judgment? (Later, I remembered what Mother said about a neighbor's husband after his wife's repeated miscarriages. "He should be castrated," she said with disdain.) Otherwise, I never had any connection or remembrance of hearing or using that word.

Each ink blot is designed to explain some area of your beliefs, and one truly explained my problem. I saw the silhouette of the devil standing on top of the earth with his arms raised above him like he had conquered the world. Then, my nightmares began.

I woke up feeling like I was looking into a black hole and the devil stood at the foot of my bed. One night, I called my counselor at 2:00 a.m. who listened to my fears and knew what to say to calm my panic and allow me to fall asleep. At the time, I thought the devil must be after me because I had strayed away from the path of righteousness. Mother's rigid beliefs wreaked havoc with my subconscious mind after I had fallen asleep.

It's also important to share that I was raised in a loving family—the love of my father and grandma. I know they loved all their children the same, but I thought I was special in their eyes. My grandma, who was in her nineties and was dying, waited until I came home from Virginia to see me. I hugged her while she kept saying my name over and over and died just moments later. I sat there and held her hand to my body until I knew I had to turn to face the family with my tears.

The story repeated with my father. Knowing he was dying, I flew home. In the nursing home, he awakened long enough to know I was there before he went into a coma. I know that people who are dying are able to wait for a loved one before they can leave this world behind, and two family members whom I loved, and who loved me dearly, waited until their death to say goodbye to me. I cannot read this without tears. They both *knew* that Mother didn't love me. Maybe that is why they gave me extra care.

My mother died a few years before this emotional trauma with the devil, but I never would have discussed it with her at any time. I did not cry at her death. When a few weeks had passed and the nightmares were gone, I was released from the exhaustion of the ordeal. Only some years later was I able to write a family history forgiving my mother and understanding the difficulties of her life after I was born.

Mother grieved for the baby she had lost just three months before I was conceived—the little boy who had lived just a few hours. Her new baby had a tendency for hyperactivity (excluding poor concentration), which created a hardship for a new mother tired from another pregnancy, another birth, and no time for recovery from the loss of her first child.

I continue to remind myself that I was not the one who created me, so why should I suffer guilt for who I was or what I did as a very young child? It's interesting that my sister and I talk about the guilt we carry around with us that is obviously from our early Christian beliefs. I feel there is something wrong with the way our mother interpreted fundamentalism, that fostered such guilt—that penetrated us like a magnet sticking to iron, even when we had moved past those earlier beliefs.

Mother and I could not talk to one another about any personal feelings. Yet, I do not remember being a disobedient child. My sister filled in—to be with mother when I said something that would bother my mother. I had an independent nature, and my mother and I didn't have loving feelings toward each other, although I wasn't consciously aware of that at the time.

Yet, I knew I had a "wild child" within who wanted to escape from rigid rules which limited my freedom to be myself. I've thought many times why my mother in the next room didn't hear me cry as a child. I know I would have been in my child's bedroom in the next minute. The wild child escaped only after the grief from my husband's death had abated when I was ready to start a new life. The following poem shares the torment that my mother faced each day.

KARMEN WORDEN

The North Window

I remember Mother at the window
to the North,
just looking out,
like she was somewhere else
other than her life on the soil
surrounded by toil
on the country farm,
forgetting the work
that would never end,
meals to fix, a garden to tend.

She dreamed of the North,
a place in the woods
by a quiet lake,
with time to meditate and pray,
watching the sunrise,
at the budding of day.
A cabin, a boat, a fishing pole,
entranced by the ripples,
how they flow,
watching the water taking
its course flowing in from some
other source, life always changing,
rearranging, like time
forever moving by.

Then Mother gave a sigh
and looked away.
Her life would always be this way.
But for a time, a tranquil picture
Filled her mind: a dream of
breaking away.

I always thought that my tears for funerals or anything like the baptism of my child were a result of the abnormality of our defective gene for depression, but this isn't true. I have been in my second marriage for many years with depression controlled with medication, and the tears continue as a part of my life. Our body's design includes this emotional range with the beautiful "highs" in life, as well as painful "lows," whether we are in the midst of depression or not. How I wish that I could have been created with a little less emotional variation like Eddie, the father of our children.

I always said that Eddie's emotional variation looked like a horizontal line. He never had highs or lows. Many times, I envied him for putting the problems of the day away and easily falling asleep with such a restful peace. He didn't bring home anxiety from his day. He didn't have thousands of inner voices thinking about all the exciting things he wanted to do next. My mind is a universe with hundreds of activities going on at the same time. I've tried to imagine this universe with different rooms with excited voices streaming out the doors—with the idea that I could close every door inside the inner inverse. It's never worked.

Maybe it really is just the differences in men and women. Men seem to be able to compartmentalize different area of their lives and not let one part of their life affect another. I visualize it as boxes. They can hear something they don't like, then they put it in a box. When I hear the same thing, my brain lights up with neon lights and every emotion link neurons throughout my whole blasted brain. We have to live our lives with the body we have been given, except for trying to change the things we are able to change.

Some of you may laugh at my tears, and I wish I could be like the man I saw interviewed on "60 Minutes" last week. The reporter was interviewing the new male Republican leader of the House of Representatives who began to weep at least five times as he answered her questions. He said, "I'm emotional. That's who I am, and everyone knows that."

What a wonderful revelation that I am not the only person on this planet troubled with tears. How I wish I could accept tears without embarrassment like our elected representative who made no apologies. Even a democrat could respect this person's forthright acceptance of his intimate nature.

Sometimes in a funeral, I count light fixtures and bricks. Now, I have to do that for my friend who taught school with me. She told me about sitting by her mother's bedside reading prayers and Bible passages as her mother lay dying. Then her mother suddenly became alert enough to ask, "Do you love the Lord?" I was moved by her story and wrote the following verse for my friend.

SOUND OF MY SONG

My Hear Has to Know

The fog pressed in
like wet snow
piled heavily on trembling
limbs,
pushing out life
grown weary from
pain and age.

Groping ahead
through the dark,
she stumbled, then paused
at the quiet voice
and the words of prayer.
It was the end, and
her child
was there.

Her voice drifted in
and then was gone
like mounds of snow
blown mercilessly
by the wind.
Waking once more,
she whispered,
"Do you love the Lord?
My heart has to know
before I can go."

KARMEN WORDEN

The answer came softly
with affirmation,
and the wind stilled.
The sun's rays
transforming flakes to droplets
only to have them vanish
like the soul,
to somewhere beyond.

The Year to Forget

Life in any family has its dark moments, but the darkness grew worse with each traumatic event this year. I felt myself drawing closer to a black hole like the one we read about in the Milky Way where everything is sucked into the depths. I had first experienced a black hole with the devil on one side during the anxiety attack I described earlier in my life. It was strange that the subconscious mind brought Mother into my consciousness requiring me to confront my issues with her when I didn't know that anything was hidden within the deep.

This paragraph summarizes that difficult year. Our son was given serious drugs for the lymphoma and had to quit the university in his last year. This was devastating for all of us. My husband's deteriorating health and emotional problems worsened, and I needed to update the antidote for the viperous gene that had attacked my brain. My depression had to be stabilized to withstand the intense pressures of stress. In May, I took the unbelievable call from my sister, Jenna, that she found her son, Jeff, in the living room, dead with a gunshot wound to his head. It is hard to feel that God is there when the pain continues one event after another, when I have prayed every day of my life for the safety of my family and for strength to care for everyone I love. My sister has prayed the same prayer.

The year began when school started in September with my own physical problems: back pain, loss of voice, and lack of energy. At Thanksgiving, my son in his last year of studying engineering at a

Virginia University, came home with a lump on his neck. He told us about the lump on his first visit home in October, but he was taking an antibiotic, which we thought would cure the infection. By Thanksgiving, the lump seemed larger, but he said he was on a second dose of an antibiotic. By Christmas break, the oncologist warned us that a biopsy must be done immediately. All the children were home when we heard the sickening news. The tumor was diagnosed as Non-Hodgkin's Lymphoma, a toxic form of lymphoma. A current of fear coursed through my body when the shock registered.

We were stunned! Our son had always been a healthy child. We couldn't believe this could be happening. Then we discovered that his chemotherapy would last for several months, and he would have to quit the university in his last year and come home for the treatments. The dark days continued through several months of continuous vomiting for three days, a few days of limited recovery, and then the treatments and sickness again. I grieved for his pain. I grieved that he had to quit school when he was in the process of interviewing for jobs. I prayed that the treatments would be a cure without damaging his body or causing him to be sterile—one possibility with this treatment. At this time, there weren't many tests to determine the doses of the chemicals that also damage the good cells. In later years, his son at age thirteen, had the same lymphoma. But with tests, they knew the right chemicals for his illness.

At the same time, my husband was struggling with the emotional stress of his failing health and the psychological strain of dealing with his mortality. We couldn't forget that he had been given three years to live after his diagnosis of congestive heart failure. Now, five years later, he had passed that marker in his life. A counselor earlier in our marriage had said that my husband's inner self was blocked like a tank—an impenetrable wall. Now, the new psychiatrist found a leak in the dike covering my husband's emotional soul, and water was seeping through the crack. I became the problem.

Now that his soul was bare, everything that was hidden could emerge in full light, and I needed the presence of mind to deal with this painful ordeal. I continued to hope that the antidepressants would keep me from entering a deep depression. I didn't know that all of this refuge existed in my husband's subconscious mind until the crack in the dike became a flood.

When people don't talk about issues, the problems aren't resolved. How can you talk to a tank?

I attended one counseling session which revealed how each of us looked at the marriage differently. During the session, the counselor gave us a problem to solve. She said, "Draw a picture revealing how you are feeling now about your relationship."

In my picture, I was hanging from the edge of a precipice with a steep drop to the rocks in a canyon below. I was holding on to the cliff with both hands while looking down at a small tree that grew out of the rocky cliff. I didn't have the strength to climb the ledge. I could drop to the tree, but it wasn't strong enough to hold me. I couldn't see any way except to drop to the depths below. My husband's picture provoked my unbelievable shock and anger. He lay flat on his back on the floor. His picture had me standing up close to his head with the toe of my shoe pressing lightly on his forehead. In the picture, he wasn't expressing any pain. His whole body looked free to move away from my foot, but he lay spread-eagled on the floor looking simply helpless and pathetic. It didn't fit the picture of our marriage from my perspective.

What kind of wife had I been? He handled all the decisions including the money in the family, except for decisions concerning the children. As a teacher, I had studied child development, and he seemed to accept that the decisions concerning the children were my specialty. Yet in the marriage, I remember saying thousands of times "Don't tell me what to do!" because I felt that he was controlling me, and I was seeking independence from his dominance.

We all know there are two sides to every story, and his would be different from mine. But truthfully, we started this relationship as teenagers both using a parent-style of interaction. It took a while to learn how to deal with each other's dominant personalities. One year of high school, I had been president of the student council, and another year he held that office. He always told me he had been a better president than I was. Maybe he was, but it was this type of competition that caused problems during the earlier years of our marriage. We learned to adjust, but that competition never really disappeared.

Next, the counselor asked what each of us thought we could do in the situation revealed by our pictures. I don't remember what my husband said as it seemed obvious to me that he should just get up off the *fricken* floor.

In my picture, I told her I couldn't see a way out. I didn't have the strength to climb the cliff and I could only fall to the rocks below. Now I wonder if it wasn't my wish to escape, or if I wanted to die. When you have depression as an unwelcome companion in your life, the thought of death is usually present in some form. Then, I heard the counselor's strange comment that still puzzles me when I think of it today. She told me to grow wings!

The high school developed a great program for teens who wanted to bring friends together to play a rock band. Both of our sons did this. Each created his own group. Only, the drummer played in our basement. I liked that they were at home creating music. Each of the groups had someone writing a song from scratch. Our second son, who would later be diagnosed with lymphoma, played guitar and his group would meet in another person's home. While Eddie was in the hospital at Richmond, our son's group with him playing the guitar won The Battle of the Bands. We were sorry we couldn't be there but happy for him that the effort to learn to play the songs on the guitar, one note at a time, paid off. He also wrote a few of the songs. The other son was happy.

"With the heart damage you have," the doctor said to Eddie and me. "You have about three years to live!" We just looked at the doctor in silence. It takes a while for this kind of news to sink in—numbness, a bolt from the blue! How could something as simple and common as a virus damage the heart! Why couldn't the doctor have recognized the problem early enough to avoid such serious complications?

Only later, I thought about our three children who were ready for college. My husband had a PhD. I was a teacher on the low-end of the salary scale. I had stayed home to take care of my children until my youngest child was in second grade—a priority for both of us. After a few weeks, with the help of the heart medications and a specialist watching his diabetes, he was able to return to work. Life moved on with each of us carrying the sorrow of a song in our hearts, knowing that whatever diversion we each could find, we could not circumvent the ending.

Teenagers can be more easily distracted, and the boys joined rock bands under the direction of the music teacher at school. One of them practiced drums in my basement, while the other spent hours on his guitar learning new music and writing his own original pieces. Teaching became my escape and respite from thoughts of my husband's illness. Throughout my teaching career, I searched for creative ideas to help children experience a love of learning through topics in social studies and through novels in reading class. I buried myself in searching for new class projects. I looked with envy at the teachers with me who went page by page in the book and left at 4:30. But I also liked my way of teaching.

Going through my files, I found this article written about twenty years ago about the effects of tears in my life and the embarrassments I've suffered when I couldn't control them. The story hasn't changed, years into the future.

Tears: Inner Strength or a Defect?

I don't know how many people have problems like mine, but my problem is tears. I cry easily, not in despair, but just about everyday things that others seem to handle without any visual evidence. I cry whenever I hear a beautiful song, attend a baptism or wedding, or hear an expression of love, a memory, or anything sentimental. I know that television characters cry without swollen eyes, without ruining makeup, and without snot running out of their noses. But my face turns red, puffy, and my eyes swell. Since the visual evidence cannot be hidden, I truly suffer when I go to a funeral.

One day, one of my teacher friends lost her mother and some of her friends and I attended the funeral. Of course when the music started during the service, the pressure began to build. I knew that controlled intervention was needed before my tears caused me embarrassment in front of my friends. I started by using this reasoning: "Susanne, this is ridiculous. You don't even know this person. She was old. It was her time to die." Then, I think of the pain my friend experiences with the loss of her mother and the tears well up again. I have compassion for her sadness.

I have devised a number of interventions, knowing as a teacher that left brain activities using numbers can trump the right brain's emphasis on emotional empathy. Besides counting bricks on the wall, I discovered that one useless bit of information kept my left brain busy. This ridiculous exercise had no value except to help me survive the funeral. I didn't need to hear the sermon.

Then one weekend, I went on a retreat for women in my church which focused on recognizing our gifts that the Lord has given us and how we can use these gifts in our daily lives. I had gone to the retreat without a conscious awareness of any gift. And obviously, I had a lesson to learn about gratitude.

After soul searching, I thought that maybe the problem of tears wasn't a problem at all. Maybe, it was a gift! I was sensitive to people and their feelings. I was awed by the beauty of creation and a Lord who had put all of it in place. I just didn't recognize this sensitivity as a gift and focused too much on my weaknesses. This was truly creative improvisation, and I was quite proud to come up with this unusual insight, even though I was determined to ask the doctor for some calming type of medication, especially for funerals.

Then, I had an interesting thought. With the unpredictability of life in this world, I only remembered one thing about heaven: there were no tears. This brought me to a matter that I needed to discuss with the Lord. I talk to the Lord like this during regular hours of the day.

"Lord," I said. I began to think about that funeral, and that got me thinking about death. Then I began to think of heaven, and the only thing I remembered was that in heaven there would be no tears. That means that I would lose this important gift. "I don't know when I'm scheduled to be there, and it's unusual to ask this kind of question. But I was wondering whether I could have another gift in its place, just an exchange, you know.

I have a little musical talent that I could use in heaven, but no voice at all. Playing the piano sounds too simplistic for a heavenly place. I really want to sing. I've heard about the beautiful heavenly chorus of angels and I'd never qualify for that chorus with my voice. So more specifically, this is my idea. I'd really like a beautiful soprano voice with a wide range like my earthly emotional highs to the depth of lows. Then maybe, if you decide this trade would be acceptable, I could try out for the Varsity Chorus—the one that travels—just in case you decide to send another chorus to earth again. It would be fun to see how my children are doing."

After my talk with the Lord, I knew quite well that this change in attitude about my gift wouldn't dry up the tears. I would get more practice in pushing left brain controls to release emotional pressure. But thinking back, it's refreshing to know that in spite of our age, we can still uncover new insights into ourselves—something that makes us unique or something that may remain hidden for some time until an event comes along to help us see more clearly what had really been there all along.

Twenty Years Later

Obviously, a lot has happened in my life since I wrote that article after finding it in one of my files. Reading this story years into the future seemed strange and my first response was to tell Maria what I thought about it.

"Susanne, the story is pathetic. Tears as a talent? I'm still living with tears and have never considered it a gift until you got that idea at a church retreat. You could have mentioned your creativity in planning lessons, in writing, or something other than what I continue to believe is an embarrassing weakness. Then, to ask for a trade with God? I know you thought you were being cute and I still talk to God today. But the 'heavenly traveling chorus?' Checking on your children?

Susanne, as my younger self, you didn't know what would happen in our future. And truly, it's a good thing that we don't know our destiny. If you cried at a stranger's funeral, you wouldn't want to know what funerals you would have to attend in future years. Later in this story, you will hear about one incident after losing our husband when he was too young to die. The other children were already in successful careers, but our youngest son in his early twenties grieved deeply about his dad's death because he didn't have time to prove himself to his father. In your story, you said you were going to try a tranquilizer for another funeral. Meanwhile, I asked my doctor for a few pills to use for our son's wedding.

Months before the wedding, I knew this celebration would be difficult for me because our son and his wife-to-be planned to include some thoughts about his dad in the wedding ceremony. Others who haven't experienced grief don't understand that important family events—the birth of a grandchild, anniversaries, and especially the wedding of a child—are painful when you know your husband would not be there.

On the day our son was to be married, my new husband Michael and I were driving to the church, and I did what I said I was going to do. I popped in a little green pill and gave it time to take effect before the ceremony. Finally, I would make it through an emotional family gathering without tears.

The wedding was beautiful and was going quite well until it came to the part where the minister would share some words about his dad. I panicked! The pill didn't seem to be working. Maybe it was wearing out because I took it too early. I was so scared of the embarrassment of losing control of my emotions because my cries can become sobs when I'm emotional. (My brother sobbed after his son's wedding was over. I liked knowing that men could also have emotions that deep.)

However, there was another fear. My new husband was sitting beside me! How could I cry like a wretched, wounded widow in front of my wonderful husband! It wasn't just the loss of my husband, but our son's reaction to his dad's death that filled me with the effects of grieving. As the pressure built, I quickly popped in a second pill.

What a mistake! I didn't cry during the wedding or the reception after the wedding as my mind was in "Za Za Land." I couldn't think clearly. Since the bride's parents knew the church and where the bride had dressed, they and the newlyweds went to the room together after the ceremony. Why wasn't I there congratulating and hugging my son? My children wondered, only to find out later that their mother was in a stupor caused by her own act. Back at the church, I didn't know where the wedding party went! What was I to do? I stood there alone, with the family pictures never entering my mind. Michael and I drove to the reception hall and waited for the wedding party.

Shouldn't it have registered with me that as the mother of the groom I shouldn't be sitting in the reception hall alone?

After the family photographs, the bridal party came back to the reception. My son immediately came over to kiss me, saying, "I thought that you knew about the pictures, Mom." Even today when I visit their home and see their wedding picture with all my children and grandchildren without my presence, my heart flips a beat. Why didn't I practice taking one or two pills ahead of time to know what kind of damage they could do? I could have had a wonderful time at the only wedding our children's father had missed. I wish my mind would never remember that incident as I beat myself up too often when I remember it.

Susanne, when I first read this story about the wedding, I planned to say that tears were a result of the abnormality of our defective gene for depression. But this isn't true. I have been in my second marriage for many years with depression controlled with medication, and the tears continue as a part of my life. Our body's design includes this emotional range with the beautiful "highs" in life as well as painful "lows," and we have to live with this body whether we are in the midst of depression or not. We are blessed with seeing the beauty of this awesome world our God has created, and our capacity to feel this joy has no limits."

Life's Joys and Sorrows

Time passed and I knew the joy of raising my children, watching them grow and develop new interests, and wondering what DNA they would inherit from their parents' genes. I believed in letting them try whatever they wanted to do and giving them a chance to develop possible interests and talents. Karen excelled in music: the piano, viola in band, and the chorus in church. Kevin wanted to make things out of wood and draw pictures, which encouraged us to sign him up for art class. After the class had finished, the teacher told me privately that Kevin had talent he should develop. He's now an engineer and develops his designs using special software on the computer. Keith was a people person, and he would excel in a job where he would interact with others.

One day, Kevin came home from kindergarten and said that everyone had to draw pictures of their families, but he said he didn't do it. "Why didn't you draw the picture? You are good in art." I knew he lacked confidence if he thought he couldn't do something very well. "Look at all the pictures you draw. Here's a piece of paper. You can draw your family without anyone else seeing you. You can go out to play when you are done." Kevin drew his picture and went outside. The next day when he came home from school, he said he drew a picture of the family, and I knew I had made the right decision in giving him the confidence he needed.

The next week at the first Back to School Night that year, we went to meet the teacher and see the children's artwork around the classroom. We walked around the room looking for Kevin's picture of his family. To my shock, he drew pictures of every single person in the family, including the dog, except his mother. He left me out of the picture. It was a lesson I never forgot. He didn't like feeling forced to draw a picture he didn't want to draw. Fortunately, I developed a wonderful relationship with this child, although I never forgot the lesson this kindergarten child taught me.

Elephant in the Room

Life in any family has its dark moments, but this particular year didn't start out very hopeful. When school started in September physical problems overwhelmed me: back pain, loss of voice, and lack of energy. "The elephant in the room." The elephant was the hidden unspoken words to a recently grieving person because no one knew how to talk about it. Well, so many painful events happened that year that it was like elephants stampeding through our household one at a time and one after another: our son was diagnosed with cancer, my husband's deteriorating health and emotional problems worsened, and my depression had to be stabilized to withstand the intense pressures of stress. Then in May, I took the unbelievable call from my sister Jenna who was sobbing that she had found her son Jeff in the living room dead with a gunshot in his head. More was to follow. It is hard to feel that God is there when the pain continues one event after another when I have prayed every day of my life for the safety of my family and for strength to care for everyone I love.

    I worried about entering the black hole again where everything in my life was swirling around and was waiting to be sucked into the depths. I had first experienced a black hole with the devil on one side during the anxiety attack I described earlier in my life. It was strange that the subconscious mind brought Mother into my consciousness, requiring me to confront my issues with her when I didn't know that anything was hidden within the deep. Yet, resolving that issue cleared that muck from my subconscious mind helping me deal with these new issues.

At Thanksgiving, my son Kevin, in his last year of studying engineering at a Virginia University, came home with a lump on his neck. Eddie blamed me for our son's use of too much alcohol at the university, because I didn't force him to go to church during his last years of high school. Eddie thought that if Keith had gone to church, he may not have started drinking at his fraternity, which made it my fault. I didn't believe in forcing church attendance on high school children, as it might turn then away from the church.

While talking to the pastor at our church, he asked Eddie if he had ever spoken to Kevin about the drinking, "Did you ever write him a letter telling him how you felt?" Eddie said he had never mentioned it. Then, the minister said, "It's not Susanne's fault if you haven't made any effort yourself to talk to your son. Go home and write him a letter, and don't blame your wife. She did what she thought was best."

Next, the counselor asked what each of us thought we could do in the situation revealed by our pictures. I don't remember what my husband said, but I remember my reaction to his picture. "Get up off the *fricken* floor!"

In my picture, I told her I couldn't see a way out. I didn't have the strength to climb the cliff, and I could only fall to the rocks below. Now I wonder if it wasn't my wish to escape, or did I want to die? When you have depression as an unwelcome companion in your life, the thought of death is usually present in some form. I had thought about which method I would use to commit suicide, but I never took it seriously. Many times in my life, I wanted to die because life was just too hard to live.

Then I heard the counselor's strange comment that still puzzles me when I think of it today. She told me to grow wings! I thought of one song of praise I had written in a program I wrote called The Rhythm of Life, and wish I could feel as I did when I wrote this verse:

Though the lightning cracks and the thunder roars,
My heart is light and my spirit soars.
I float on air like a bird with wings,
Upward, upward, my spirit sings.

We catch a current
Then start to rises
Past towers and steeples
Up, up through the skies.
We drift. We glide,
And our heads feel light
As we float on past
The wispy clouds of white.

So life goes on
For the human race
As the earth moves round,
In time and space.
From dawn to dusk
From night to day,
The clock ticks on
As the children play.

Was This the Plan?

Way down under,
deep, deep below
the conscious thoughts
of things we know,
lies the conglomeration
of all that's new:
each whoop-de-do
and hullabaloo
of this very day,
play by play.

Each
illogical inspiration,
ridiculous reverberations,
absurd analysis,
paranoid paralysis,
all mixing and turning,
grinding and churning,
trying to fit
all these new crazes
into past files and
network of
mazes.

Dear Lord,
It can't be true
that you planned it this way,
that the mixture is quiet
all through the day,
and then in the evening
after I've counted the sheep,
the mixture starts creepin'
and leapin' down deep
just when I'm desperate
for a good night
of sleep?

KARMEN WORDEN

Called The Rhythm of Life

The symphony of nature
Was alive with song
With the rhythm of change
As life moves along.

Weeping willows
Clouds like fluffy pillows
Buds changing to flowers
Fine mist to showers
So the legacy of man
Is a questioning, a burning
To understand the life we know,
Our spirits, forever yearning.

Growing Wings?

I know that just because I do not feel the Spirit, that doesn't mean that the Spirit isn't working within me. I think the counselor's message was a fanciful way to tell me to rise above my problems. In normal circumstances, it would be a creative idea. But was my life normal? I had begun a master's degree in teaching prospective teachers Math education, and obviously, I had to quit to help my husband through his crisis. However, I could not change how my son's cancer penetrated the "Mother Nurturing Center" in my brain. My husband in my first marriage had never understood my depression nor did he ever know how to respond to me in a way that gave me comfort.

When I dealt with the grief from my son's cancer, it affected every cell in my body.

Our marriage suffered during this painful year, and I was quite over my head: teaching school, being present for my son, trying to handle back pain that resulted from the effects of the thyroid problem, and the tense atmosphere in our home. My husband talked to other men at work, and he shared personal information with them. I was embarrassed that my husband may be sharing such details about me that should be private. I wondered, is this what happens to men in a mid-life crisis? They look back and try to find out what they had missed in their past life?

Unfortunately, my brain couldn't wing its way from my son who was ill. My brain couldn't take to the air from my husband who was trying to live with the knowledge of his death. At this time, I wished I could feel the Spirit within.

Yet, I know the counselor meant it in a different way. Instead of growing wings, I could emotionally soar above the problem and see it in a different light. My husband was getting help for his mid-life crisis which could change his attitude about the years we had left together. My son had good doctors who were giving him medications that could save his life. Maybe, when it was over, he would go back to school, complete his degree, and begin again to search for a job.

In the midst of all these problems, I could not wing my way to a positive outlook of the problem I faced. Looking back at the past, I wish I could have risen above the problems facing me, but it isn't a feeling that can be plucked out of the air at the time of a crisis.

Learning About Suicide

But the story of our family had just begun. When one believes that the darkness could not become more dense, my sister Jenna called in May with the tragic news about her son. She came home from teaching school and found him sitting on the couch with a gun between his knees and a bullet wound in his forehead. This handsome and popular eighteen-year-old child was finishing high school, had just ordered a tuxedo for the prom, and had been accepted at three different universities. With dread and unbelief that this could be happening, I left my sick son and my husband with the leaking dike bursting like a waterfall over a dam, and flew home to be with Jenna and her family.

No words can describe the depth of this pain, the unreality that this could be possible, and the decisions that had to be made even with the wrenching agony of the grief. So many friends waited in line for the viewing that the line extended around the building outside. Thankfully, my medication kept me sane and capable of caring for my sister and her family. I was able to put my own feelings aside to be there for my grieving sister.

Throughout the year after Jenna's son died, she and each of the children needed counseling to help them through the grieving process. Later, she began studies at the university and finished with a degree in counseling. She said that in all her studies of depression, most people in the field felt that suicide was an impulsive act, one that could have been avoided, although this should not cause grief for loved ones left behind. The circumstances sometimes cannot be changed.

Jenna felt that if she had come home a few minutes earlier, if the telephone had rung during that time, or if someone had dropped by, that moment of desperation could have passed. He told her he had been having headaches and Jenna had made an appointment with the doctor the very next day, but he killed himself before he could see the doctor. The act of suicide isn't always one that has been premeditated. Someone can decide in one moment that life isn't worth living, and without thinking of anything else, he or she jumps into the steaming geyser, unaware how seriously that act will impair the lives of everyone who had ever known or loved him.

Antidepressants do not relieve grief. Grief flowed through every cell of my body penetrating the neurons within. Antidepressants help you become the normal person you were born to be without the default of this defective gene. My normal self returned only if I was on the right medication to balance the neurotransmitters in my brain. Even with depression, we have the capacity to recover and survive unbelievable hardships. We humans are more resilient than we think we can be.

When I came home from the funeral, I learned that more was still to come. It was Mother's Day and my husband said he wanted to take me for a ride in the afternoon. My mind couldn't concentrate on anything else but the funeral. I felt suspicious that he would take me somewhere else to talk, but he drove to a quiet spot and stopped the car. Then he dumped the rest of the dirty water from the bottom of the dike on my head and said how quiet and peaceful it was when I was gone. He had been thinking about it during that week and he thought he wanted a divorce.

I was too numb to remember what I said or did, except to come home and call my children in tears telling them what had happened. Thankfully, nothing came of this discussion as he never mentioned it again. I know this was the final breakdown after all of his sessions with the psychiatrist. Eventually, he was able to live with the knowledge of his mortality and work almost to the very end of his life which would come just a few years later.

The experience with the psychiatrist helped Eddie realize that he had a wall between the real world and his emotional soul on intimate, emotional issues. Once in a discussion, Eddie said he couldn't come up with an answer immediately and it would take a day or two before he could think of how he wanted to respond. He had no problems expressing his opinions on other impersonal subjects.

The first counselor who talked to both of us at the first session of marriage counseling said he couldn't work with Eddie, only with me. My emotions could easily be expressed, discussed, and possibly resolved. The counselor wondered if the loss of Eddie's teenage brother when Eddie was only four seriously affected his life. Younger children, not understanding grief, sometimes think they are the cause of problems in the family. Another family member told me that Robert's death was never discussed by a single person in the family as if it never happened. The children got up the next morning as if Robert had never existed. In addition, their father suffered a deep depression after his son's death, which worried the family, and no doubt didn't help Eddie get the attention he needed during these impressionable years.

Today, with more knowledge about stages of grief through books and articles published, we know that it helps most people to share their feelings and discuss the problems they face. For those of us who are open with our feelings, it is hard to understand how the death of a child would not be a subject to share with other members of the family.

Somehow, we have the strength to survive whatever happens in our lives, knowing that even with all the grief, pain, and death of our loved ones, many of us continue to live a blessed life. Today's children and grandchildren don't know poverty. Like me, they live in a beautiful home and have luxuries that others couldn't imagine. Now, medical research carries new treatments for diseases that were not possible even a year ago. How can I feel anything except thanks to God for each day of blessings? I appreciate that my work load has been lessened, work that my ancestors did with hard labor.

Whenever I feel sorry for myself because of my depression or arthritic pain, I remember my great grandpa who was bedridden for twenty years from rheumatoid arthritis. The funeral director thought he would have to break his bones to fit him into a casket. I can't even imagine the pain he suffered without the medication we have today. That memory can put my life's problems today in the proper perspective.

The most significant book that one can read, if one is prone to despair, is the book Man's Search For Meaning by Viktor Frankl, a writer and psychotherapist who survived four concentration camps including Auschwitz. Frederick Netzsche wrote about Frankl saying, "Even in the degradation and abject misery of a concentration camp, Frankl was able to exercise the most important freedom of all—the freedom to determine one's own attitude and spiritual well-being. No sadistic Nazi SS guard was able to take that away from him or control the inner-life of Frankl's soul."

Everything seems dark when I read my story, but I have to tell you about the other side of our lives: and that is the need to find new love, and this could take months even years. First is the need to go out of the house. Even that is painful at first, but it's easier to find a friend to go with you. We meet at lunch or a bar nearby. Then we order a drink, and giggle to each other (if we're in a bar) and I say. "We're just practicing our single lives." I found a friend, and we would go out together. It's much easier to be with a friend. Thinking of it that well helped me add humor to it and makes it neither good nor bad, as we have to practice dealing with that, too.

Depression Strikes Again in My Brother's Family

I explained earlier how depression runs in families and that depression would affect each of our three children's families. My story has covered the two of my parent's children: my sister's child, Jeff, and me. But depression hadn't skipped my brother Jack's family. Jack has a bright son, Paul, who graduated from a university with a degree in economics and marketing. He found a good job in Chicago, and seemed to be very successful—until he disappeared from his work and didn't answer his home phone.

Jack drove to the city looking for him, but Paul had moved and left no forwarding address. Jack called different people who might know where Paul could be but to no avail. Jenny searched the Internet trying to find a way to locate him there. We lived with the knowledge that something had seriously happened to Paul.

Close to two years of agony after their son disappeared, Paul called for his dad to come to the city to bring him home. He was like the prodigal son—dirty, with no driver's license, no money, and he refused to share what had happened to him. To this day, he won't discuss the problem. He's on medication for depression prescribed by an internist. He continues to live and work with his dad at home on the farm. Our family hopes that he will recover to live the kind of normal life he wants and needs.

I know that many other problems make it difficult to find the proper help.

1. When someone quits or loses a job, he loses his health insurance.
2. Without a driver's license, he cannot drive.
3. Some people live in a town far away from a city where help is not available. My brother lives fifty miles from the nearest town with good medical services.
4. When people don't have the money to provide the help that is needed, then they cannot use their talents and gifts God has given for their lives.

For me, the many serious trauma in our family in the 1989 episodes simply broke down my guard rail of security like pealing back an onion to the tender core. Antidepressants will always be necessary for my health, similar to a diabetic needing insulin. I picture the medications like workers in my brain dumping on the right substances every day to keep the core healthy.

I am also sincerely thankful that I have taken advantage of all the psychiatrists who have helped me, and for the medications that have made it possible for me to raise my children, to teach school, and to live a normal life in spite of this mental condition. Now in my later years, I researched and wrote the history of my Swedish and Norwegian side of the family. Because the children lost their grandpa before they were born, they will never know the love he had for his children. This made it necessary for me to write the German family history, too. My husband had three brothers and a sister, and I asked them to write me about his childhood. I did what I could to leave a legacy that they will appreciate as they grow older.

I hope my story doesn't sound so tragic that you can't believe that you can carry on with your life, but we humans are resilient and can recover from any problem with the help of God. I thank God for the ability to continue my work, and enjoy my children and now my grandchildren.

Premonitions of Future Events

After the funeral of my nephew, the family searched the room thoroughly looking for a note written by their son. If only they could know why he would have done this terrible thing. Later, Jenna kept hearing an inner voice when she'd go upstairs, "Look under the pencil box. Look under the pencil box." She ignored it many times as they had searched the room thoroughly. One day, she walked into the room and looked under the pencil box in his desk. To her shock, she found the letter. She said I could read the letter, but being on antidepressants myself, I couldn't read the letter. It was better for me not to know the terrible symptoms of depression that he expressed in the letter. It was better for me never to know the agony he must have felt to take the step that would haunt his family forever. Jenna hadn't recognized any different behavior in the past weeks.

Of course, Jenna and the three children needed individual family counseling. And what is often the case with these family traumas, her marriage fell apart. People grieve in different ways. When one feels the other should just "get over it," then the marriage can't work. Later, after Jenna finished a master's degree in counseling, she contacted all parents who had lost children to help them through their grief. She has been an inspiration to many people who felt they couldn't have made it through the death of a child without her guidance and support.

A strange incident happened when my sister, brother, and I stayed by our father's bed as he lay dying. He was in a coma and could no longer hear us, we thought. But we continued to sit by his bed, hold his hands, talk to him, and let him know how much we loved him.

Then my sister Jenna said, "Where is that music coming from?" My brother and I couldn't hear any music. It felt very strange and I wrote the following poem to remember it forever. It is not good poetry, but I include it as it expresses exactly what happened that day when Jenna heard music when my brother and I heard nothing at all. This poem explains the story.

The Heavenly Song

"Our Father, who art in Heaven, hallowed be Thy Name,"
Over and over, his prayer was the same.
He prayed in the morning and all through the day.
Our daddy's life was breaking away.

Somehow he knew that his dying was near,
For he loved the Lord and had nothing to fear.
He wanted no more to desperately pray,
"Dear Lord, I am ready. Please take me today."

As we siblings sat by our father's bed,
"Where is the music?" our sister said.
The band is practicing, I heard myself say.
But then I remembered it was no longer day.

As I looked at my brother with a bit of surprise,
Seeing the questioning as well in his eyes,
"Check the next door or out in the hall,"
For my brother and I heard nothing at all.

Then our daddy died and we left the room,
While his body was washed, the hearse coming soon.
Out in the hall, my whispers were low,
"Do you hear the song now?" But she shook her head, "No."

This foreseeing the future had happened before,
When she dreamed a child died before it was born.
We know when we held Daddy's hand the night long,
That our sister had heard the heavenly song.

My Feelings during a Depression

When I am in the grips of depression, the fog creeps in and the song of my life is temporarily hidden away. I am alive, but my shadow seems to take charge. What happened to my dreams of writing a book? They are under the surface. My *skep* (skeptical) is my critic who is always ready to tell me that I can't write anything that someone would want to read, which is tragic. Writing is the passion where I lose myself for hours when I feel well. I think having a passion is critical to recovery.

My self-image slips to the depths. It's like knowing you can play a song for the piano recital perfectly because you have practiced it so many times. Now, in the midst of depression, you are aware that people are looking at you. It is possible you will forget a section or your hands will shake, leaving you unable to play the piece perfectly like you have done so many times before. Your insecurities and self-consciousness slip into your life.

In a depression, I am very tired. I don't want to go to the book club. I don't want to go to the theater, or to potlucks or to the clubhouse for classes. I need to call my psychiatrist and ask to see her again. What medication could I add to bring me back to a normal state?

People cannot say, "Get over it! Think of all the blessings you have!" I am so well aware of the blessings in my life. If I could control how I feel and make the changes, I would have learned to do it by now. If it is the chemistry in my brain, then medications change my attitude, and I thank God each day for the wonders of feeling like myself. I am thankful that my brain generates so many ideas that I feel I need a longer life to get everything done.

I believe the Lord has given each of us talents (I call gifts.) which fit our body and mind. When we die, our soul brings our story back to God. It's saying to God, "This is how I used the gifts you gave to me." Developing a passion like writing has always carried me away from the present, taking me into the inner world of the story or project I was creating. During my marriage to Eddie, It helped to forget that Eddie's and my life together could end at any time. We simply didn't talk about his future. Eddie took shots every day for diabetes, and I took pills to normalize the chemicals in my brain.

My doctor selected medications that worked for me. These medications are different for everyone because of the different chemicals in our brains that cause depression. One chemical, serotonin, contributes to feelings of well-being plus other functions like regulating mood and helping with memory and learning. My doctor explained that my medication has two different chemicals, and if I'm not on the right medication, one of those two chemicals could be missing.

The Wrong Medication

Psychiatrists have been trained in the use of these medications and there's no test to determine which chemical works for an individual person. The doctor may need to try different types of medications and watch out for the results which may take a few weeks to have an effect. If the patient feels no change in the depression, then another kind of medication can be substituted. I had a relapse in depression at two different times of my life because I had taken the wrong medications.

The first time this happened, I had asked my internist if he could prescribe an antidepressant instead of going to the psychiatrist every year to refill the drug. During that time, I saw her only for the medications. In fact, she did needlework during the session and still charged me $200 an hour. It was like going to a tea party. My internist agreed to prescribe my medications and wrote out a prescription for Prozac, a popular drug on the market.

It wasn't but a week or two later when I suddenly felt wonderful. I thought, "Susanne, you finally have gotten your life all together again." I didn't need as much sleep, and I was so excited about the writing that when a new idea came to me in the night, I'd get up at 3:00 a.m. to work on the article. Then I had to get up to teach school the next morning. It was such a productive and electrifying time of my life for about a month—until I hit a terrible low.

I continued to teach school, but I knew I was in the deepest depression I had ever experienced. The Second Face of Susanne, who had always handled classroom students, working with other people working with me, but inside my body, my self-image suffered. Then I encountered a problem with one student who disliked me. I asked the principal to take him out of my class, but she refused and sent me to the counselor who called all the parties into her room. I knew that in my low period, I cried easily, and I could fly which would make it difficult to face the counselor, the parents and the child in her tiny office.

The counselor planned a counseling session with the child, his parents, and me. I became so upset during the session and feared that I would embarrass myself by crying in front of a student and his parents that I walked out of the conference. A teacher simply doesn't walk out of a conference. I wanted the child out of my class, but the principal wouldn't allow that change. I continued to teach with the child in my class. I was only happy when the manic cycle swung high, and I could climb on my flying trapeze and rise above earthly problems while singing the joyful song, "Joy to the World and the deep blue sea, joy to you and me." (Lyrics by Hoyt Axton)

I went back to my psychiatrist to explain my manic attacks, and she immediately changed my prescription to the one that had previously worked effectively. However, the cycles of highs and lows didn't disappear until several months later when I started the new medication. I continued to cycle monthly—a month in the manic highs to a month of living in the depths. This continued for several months, although none of the cycles were as severe as the first one. The cycles had to gradually wear down before they disappeared forever. Prozac is a miracle drug for some people. But for me, it was a nightmare for half of my teaching year.

All medications have side effects—some may make you sleepy or edgy, or another kind of side effect could appear. The doctor needs to know the side effects to determine whether you are on the right mediation. But minor side effects are unimportant if you cannot live a normal life without them. I had no side effects with the antidepressant that worked effectively for me, except for a greater sense of hyperactivity which I learned to live with.

There was no possibility of addiction to any of the drugs I have taken. My greatest need during depression, besides being on the right medication, was to always share my feelings. But the only safe place to talk about my feelings was with my sister Jenna by phone, since we lived across the country from one another. The stigma may be improving, but most of us with depression are fearful to share our depression with any group.

One time in a book club meeting, where we discussed the depression of one of the characters in the book, I told them for the first time that I took medication for depression. The next month after the meeting of the book club, a member called me and the conversation went this way: "What was wrong today? Were you feeling okay? You didn't seem like yourself." I told her I was feeling fine. I have no idea why she called except at the last meeting when I shared that I take medication for depression, she was watching me during this meeting to see if I acted differently.

> I have been sorry ever since I shared this personal story. Finally, I had to quit the group. I learned that you can't tell anyone except loved ones who would know the story of your life.

Taking in a University Student

In the next few years before my husband's death, he was able to enjoy several momentous family celebrations including our daughter's wedding and graduation from medical school. Then our son, having recovered from lymphoma and graduated from the university that summer, married a Japanese student studying at a nearby university. After offering her our home to learn about another country through the eyes of a foreign student, our house guest joined our family when she and our son married. During this time, my husband's diabetes turned worse. He used crutches for months at a time with sores on his feet that didn't heal. Also, side effects from so many medications caused other heart problems.

Hope with Experimental Drug

When we heard about a new experimental drug advertised as a breakthrough for congestive heart failure, Eddie signed on to be a part of the blind study to decide which of two dosages would result in the greater success. We were warned about the danger of the drug: the drop in the level of white blood cells which would affect his immune system, and weaken his body to withstand colds and other illnesses. The white blood cells had to be checked each week.

After coming home from one last trip to visit friends and family in the Middle West, the trip to the doctor resulted in shocking news with a white blood count of zero. He was admitted to the hospital, never to return home. I will never forget how long he sat in the waiting room, knowing his life was over. He didn't want to go to his room with the nurse, and I'm so sorry I didn't go with him and the nurse upstairs. Then I would have been with them to *stop* them from putting him on the machines. But this was a trial, and of course, they didn't want other deaths with this study. My daughter, a doctor of internal medicine, said that the drug never got to the market.

Our sons came to the hospital immediately. But our daughter, a physician in another state who couldn't come home so soon, talked to us and the doctors by phone. The health care document stated that he did not want to be kept alive on machines if death was imminent. But between the time we saw him in the lobby until we walked in the room, he had gone into a coma and had already been attached to the machine that was keeping his body temporarily functioning. My two sons, daughter-in-law, and I stood by his bed in shock. The doctor said that nothing more could be done to save him. We stood there in silence, knowing we had to eventually make the painful decision to disconnect the mechanism that was keeping him alive.

When death is near for a loved one, thankfully, the Lord created a brain that responds with numbness to help us deal with the shock of death. I shared my story of tears for beautiful moments, for inspirational stories, and for the death of a stranger. Now, I stood next to my husband's bed and prayed the twenty-third psalm aloud, close to his face, and without a single tear. Then the machine was turned off. I placed my hand on his stomach, feeling it change from warm to cold. I do not remember who took me home or what happened next. My brain was frozen in time.

Expressing My Grief through Poetry

The poem "Darkness in the Valley" describes the many different thoughts I had after his death. Not all of these thoughts and feelings came at once, but all of them were natural and normal at some time during the grieving experience. Anger came as a first response.

A couple in church lost a daughter to suicide. The mother was very angry and they quit the church. I sent her an e-mail asking how our members could have helped her. She said that no one had cared enough to say they were sorry that she had lost her daughter. She said that in church when we pass the peace (greeting those around us with "peace be with you"), we all do the act, yet no one cared about her.

You can't short circuit grief. There's no way around it. You have to feel it, live through it, and grieve before you are ready to move on. A few months after my husband died, I facilitated a support group with my church providing a room for the weekly meetings. There, widowed people can discuss anything about their grief and know that everyone will understand. A few people stayed in the group for three years, because they continued the need to talk about their loneliness.

One time, a young man joined our group. He shared the guilt he felt about wanting to meet someone else. He needed someone in his life to share his love and the love for his two young children. I asked him if he loved his first child less after his second child was born. "Of course not," he said, and he never came back. I felt that my comment helped him or he may have realized that he didn't need the group. Sometimes, people need a different way to look at their shattered lives before they can move on.

The easiest way to express my pain more deeply about grieving came through writing poetry. Words came more easily to me in that genre. The following poems expressed the different aspects of my grief, especially guilt or remembering something I wish I wouldn't have done or said. Of course, I feel like I am just one-half of a person. The other part of me is gone and dead. How could I ever feel the same again?

The truth of the matter is that we will no longer be the same. Every change in our lives has an impact on our lives today, as well as our future. We need to deal with the pain of *now*. Most of our married life, the music played out as songs of joy for the values we shared, the love we had for one another, and the beauty of raising our children and watching them develop.

KARMEN WORDEN

Darkness in the Valley

I am in the Valley of Grief,
The foggy meadow
   hidden from view
Overpowered by the
   massive mountain
That lies before me,
   and I know that I
Tread this path alone.
   There is no way
Around, no path to
   follow, no way over
The top. Only the climb,
   one step at a
Time, to arrive at the other side.

They say that time will
   ease my pain,
And the trickle of fluids
From the raw wound
Will no longer weep
   and my body
Discard the oozing
   matter as tears.
Will the climb, one
   step at a time, be
Counted in moment
   upon moment
For years upon years?

I am vaguely aware of others
Out there who know
   of my pain,

And they turn to me and smile.
"You are doing so well," they say.
But they really would
   like to forget.
They really don't want to know
That life is so fleeting,
And death stalks closely behind.
My life is just a reminder.

In the Valley of Grief,
   I reflect upon
Those last moments of his life
Etched in permanent stone.
The mechanical means that kept
The lungs breathing, the heart
Beating, the blood flowing,
Had to be withdrawn,
Allowing the spirit to flee back
To the place from where
   it had come.

Like a switch that slows
   the flow of
Power to a light, the
   circuits in my
Brain switched into numbness
To ease the shock of death,
   and I could whisper
Those comforting words
   of the Twenty-third
Psalm, as he walked into

SOUND OF MY SONG

"The valley of death, to
   dwell in the House of
The Lord forever."

And when I entered the
   Valley of Grief, it was
Then that I wished
And wished I could know
As a sure thing, that it
   really existed;
This "House of the
   Lord forever."
What if death is only death?
And life is only life,
And there is no more hereafter,
And my hope and faith
   are all in vain?

In the loneliness of my
   valley, I hear
The sound of his voice,
The footsteps in the
   hallway. I sense
The smell of his presence on the
Pillow next to mine. I weep for
What we have lost. Our dreams
Ended with his death,
And I begin a new life, alone.

My valley is a colorless world,
A place where fog plays
   hide and seek
With the sun, but the sun hides,
Keeping the sparkle
   of light away
As I entered the world of Gray.
Like a boat man at
   home with the sea
Wandering barefoot in
   the desert sun,
I wander in my valley alone.
I don't belong to anyone.

KARMEN WORDEN

Numb from the Predator's Blow

Like a predator tears at its kill,
The loss of my love tears at my soul.
I am broken, not whole,
Cold like the kill,
Too numb to cry out in pain.
My cries to the Lord
Seem all in vain.

Hurt words I've said
Float up to the surface
Of my mind like smoke
Rising from a fire,
While tender words of love,
Laughter, and fun,
All are smothered below.

If only this! If only that!
If only I'd known,
I'd have watched my words.
But now I'm alone
With memories replaying.
The sad songs linger
And crowd out praying.

Tears rise and flow.
If only they would
Wash out the guilt
And cleanse my soul.
But no! My mind's a
One-track show,
Numb from the predator's blow.

The Seashell

I walk alone on the beach,
    waves crashing on shore,
    then receding, leaving behind
    a single shell
    awash in the
    sand.

I stop to examine the seashell,
    once a safe, solid shelter
    supporting a beating heart within,
    protected, like my life
    before I was left
    alone.

Little Clam, you were once like me,
    snug in your shell
    at the bottom of the sea,
    innocently unaware
    of your
    destiny.

Now, chipped and cracked,
    your weakened shell flakes,
    gradually mingling
    with grains of sand
    becoming at one
    with the
    sea.

But, as for me,
    my heart still beats
    cherishing memories
    of yesterday,
    yet looking ahead
    with hope
    to what might
    be.

SOUND OF MY SONG

The Dance

From where does it come,
this sensation of drum,
The reveling sound
in the night, all around,
a rhythmic beat
by a fireside heat,
the rum tum tum tum
of a primitive drum!

The night fills with sound,
with laughter around.
The stirring of danger,
the smile of a stranger.
I dance till I'm numb
with the beat of the drum,
like an impulsive child
untethered and wild.

Are they sounds from afar
that rattle and jar,
or are they within
just under my skin?
Passions run deep,
for I sense in my sleep
the strain of a song
that makes my heart long.

Are these my dreams?
So real it seems,
these sounds of the night
before the daylight,
enraptured, entranced
from the heat of the dance,
and the rum tum tum tum
of the primitive drum!

Identity Crisis

I never thought I'd need advice,
but thinking alone, doesn't seem to suffice.
It helps to talk, to have some support
from friends who wait for another report
of where I'm at in this day of my life,
now that I'm single and nobody's wife.

It's my first time alone after his sickness
and death, yet I know in this life I've been very
much blessed. I'm painfully aware
that I'm experiencing grief,
and to know he's not suffering,
is a definite relief.
They say it takes time; this I know
very well, so I joined up with friends.
We're all living in hell.

I talk in the group of the problems I face,
now that I'm single in this time,
in this place, managing myself,
completely alone with an identity crisis
that's become full blown.
Before this time, we were always a "we"
in the familiar marriage mentality.

His job was his, and my job was mine,
and our lives were going along just fine.
He was used to my moods,
when I'd rant and rave, and I accepted
his need for time in the cave.
We shared all the plans, sometimes with a fuss,
but, all of the decisions were made by us.

SOUND OF MY SONG

Just like in our teens, we didn't know
who we were and our lives sometimes
seemed like a dark, murky blur.
We wanted that time
of our lives to be past
when our identity crisis would be over
at last. Never dreaming one day
in a future unknown, we'd be facing
the same kind of crisis
full blown.

Now the moral of this story is
one I must share:
Having your life all in order
is a plan—very rare.
Just when you think you have turned
a new page,
this dilemma couldn't happen
to anyone your age.
When life becomes quiet
and peaceful, it's then
An identity crisis may be just
around the bend.

The Ripple

There is beauty in the thought
that because of something today,
someone I met,
some new idea,
reflection,
recollection,
a rare find,
a word of encouragement,
a special gift,
a new way to look at something old,
a thought of what could somehow be
an enlightening possibility
could change the way
I view my life
Tomorrow.

A Message to My Deceased Husband

My friend Ann said with delight,
That her husband came to her last night.
If that is true, then I cannot see
Why you haven't appeared to me!

If you are now in a spirit state,
Allowed out of the heavenly gate,
Your body now not earthly-bound,
Appear to me when you're around!

I'd like you to know that I am well,
Though grief has been a living hell.
I want another message clear,
I'm spittin' mad you left me here.

Confusion

I wrote that note on a paper scrap.
Now I can't remember where it's at.
I'm going out, I need to know.
Where is the place I was to go?

I search in the closet for gloves to wear,
But I cannot find a single pair.
Oh yes, gloves! I see three,
All as different as can be.

When I'm driving in my car,
Before I've gone so very far,
I become alert! I think I'll cry!
I just discovered I drove on by.

There are other things I do as well,
That I'm not so very proud to tell.
I can't remember what clothes I wore
Or when I dusted or mopped the floor.

So many details fly on by,
But now I know the reason why.
I read in a book, such a relief,
"Memory loss is caused by grief!"

My Play

I am the director of my play.
The actor, choreographer,
the writer with no lines,
no queues,
no script to tell me what to do.
Each moment is part of a different scene,
discouraging hopes,
or encouraging dreams.

I'd like a change. Is it a risk
like looking into a deep abyss?
A new plan with a different twist,
that's what I've missed.
Exploring what I've never done,
taking a chance to have some fun.
So I can say to this new plot,
"Dull, it's not."

Yet there are boundaries
in my play.
Although I wish that I could say
that the boundaries don't exist.
This would be my life's old twist.
Walls through which I cannot pass
are in my life. Alas! Alas!
My inner voice is there to say,
"No you can't do that today,
not tomorrow, or any day."

KARMEN WORDEN

But maybe this isn't the very last word,
for another voice there
cries to be heard.
What would the matter be,
if I stepped outside of the boundary?
It doesn't mean I'd have to stay.
I could change my mind another day.
"Don't be so rigid. Let yourself loose,"
I tell myself, to give me a boost.
I'll try a plan with a different twist.
As I said before,
that's what I've missed.

SOUND OF MY SONG

Written for a Cave Man Rap when "early man" dealt with the earth and fear of storms. Sometimes, widowed people can feel like this.

>The animals howl.
>The air smells so foul.
>What danger befalls me this night?
>The sky looks so gray.
>It's not far away.
>I feel more safe when it's light.
>
>The air flips and flails.
>It flattens and wails.
>It pounds me with its fury.
>It freezes and fouls.
>It hammers and howls.
>I'm funky with fear and worry.
>
>It flings me around
>And flattens the ground.
>Where can I go to be free?
>I'm fraught with fright.
>I cry in the night.
>I haven't got time to flee.

KARMEN WORDEN

The storm fritters away
Till another day.
It scampers. I know not why.
The air smells so clear.
The birds lose their fear,
As they soar up into the sky.

The earth comes alive.
The land did survive,
And creatures peek out from the stubble.
The plants dry their tears
And forget all their fears,
As new life begins from the rubble.

Blown with the Wind

I do not know who I am.
I am like a leaf
caught in the morning breeze,
rolling this way and tumbling that,
blown about with the wind.
I want my former life
when I was alive and vibrant,
not dull brown, wilted, and desolate.
A time when sap from the roots
nourished my veins,
not vulnerable to the forces without,
when the impact of nature
did not have the power
to shake my spirit.

One day, I know not when,
I felt a movement within.
I was not dead,
not a wilted leaf caught
powerless by forces
I could not see.
New life, vibrant and alive,
once again flowed from deep
within the earth, powered
by spring rays of the sun.
Then, sad memories of the night
changed to become
the hopefulness
of light.

The Awakening

Death strikes, leaving a life left behind,
Enclosed like a cocoon in darkness.
Seeking not, hoping not in the grip of grief,
Like a plant wilted from drought, leaves
Curled, protecting itself from the scorching sun,
Vulnerable to the forces without.

A cry for life as it was before. The comfort
Of continuity, the security of what was known.
Someone had cared and shared my dreams.
Time passed, time to be reflective. One day,
I knew that grief had colored my soul,
How the view of my life had been out of perspective.

In the stillness of night, a stirring within,
A sensation of change flowed through my veins,
Like a rosebud gripped tightly before it's
Future came clear, "Open your petals to the sun,
Feel the breeze caress your tender skin."
Like the gentle petals of rose, I knew an
Awakening within.

The flow of nourishment filled my soul.
The grip of grief releasing its power.
My life never again the same,
Since the passing of this hour. A cocoon.
Life seeming to die, a chrysalis forms,
Then a butterfly, shedding the shroud
Of darkness, like me, with wings to find
My destiny.

My Tree

I am a leaf,
with a dull brown surface.
Dried crisp and torn
rolling here and tumbling there
in the early, chilly, autumn morn.
Caught in the spirals and swirls,
I perceive the end,
threatened by mere whispers
of the wind.

I grew upon a massive oak.
Roots plowed deep within the earth
gaining strength since my sapling birth.
Limbs held strong when gusts and gales,
and harsh, tough cries,
of stern wind wails
would threatening be
to my massive tree.

One day, when the days grew short,
and the nights came cool,
my sap would be the sacrifice.
Drawn back within the tree,
the oak would live, instead of me.
When gusts and gales, and harsh,
tough cries of stern wind wails,
would threatening be
to my massive tree.

KARMEN WORDEN

Now my oak digs deep
into the ground searching for nourishment
from below, gaining strength before the snow.
But as for now, my time is past
while my tree withstands
the strong wind blasts.
Soon, my legacy will be
a part of the sustenance
for my tree.

Is it possible that our lives will be
like the leaves upon the tree?
Our legacies, the sustenance for our souls
when we've fulfilled our earthly roles.

Wild Child Rattles the Chains

Since a good friend Kelly and I were in our respective third year after the loss of our husbands, we had been going to the support group each week for over two years. Now, when we were ready to move on, we chose a bar and restaurant near our house where we could sit at a table by ourselves and talk, have a drink, order food, or watch others dancing. I had a glass of wine and Kelly drank Perrier, since her husband had been an alcoholic. Neither of us had ever been to a bar. It wasn't part of our marriages, and we knew that hanging out in bars would not be part of our future lives. But we needed a place to go regularly to feel like we were exercising our single status.

The first night we walked in, we were uncomfortable but pretended that this was a perfectly natural thing for us to do. We both knew we were allowing a different part of our personalities to escape for a brief moment, although Kelly preferred to look at men and want to see a little boy with sparkling eyes and the capability of mischief, the attributes she loved in her husband.

"What are we doing here?" Kelly asked, looking around at the people who didn't fit our experience of quality men we would be comfortable with anywhere else we would go. We knew we weren't looking for a date or even a friend in this setting. We were like giggly teenagers, thinking we were doing something improper yet playful. I wouldn't have wanted to see a church member I knew coming into the bar.

"We're practicing our new single life," I answered. "How can we do anything new without practice?" Kelly would laugh at the very thought of it. "Remember, we were the generation who married young. Not like today when our kids began careers, delaying marriage and children."

Kelly said, "We never lived life alone."

"When I married on my twentieth birthday, my husband was nineteen," I said. "I rode with his parents to get a license because he was still too young to sign the marriage certificate. At that age, my children were freshmen in college with years ahead of them to enjoy life before they married."

"At least, we'll be tired tonight when we go home to our empty house," Kelly said. We both disliked going home to an empty house. One night, I was scared. As I opened the door of the garage to the kitchen, I remembered that I had not locked the sliding glass door to the basement. Our house backed up to trees and a creek in the back. Anyone could have entered my house. I looked in the garage for an axe, but remembered that when Eddie died, I had given it to my son.

If I were going to search the whole house, I needed a weapon, and the largest weapon I had was a huge hammer. Feeling fearful, I started in the basement. After locking the back door, I searched every closet, behind the shower curtains, the main floor, upstairs under every bed, and in every closet. Only when I knew I had covered the whole house could I put my hammer down, and relax. But adrenaline was still running wild, and I couldn't get to sleep right away.

Kelly and I continued to go to the bar some weekend nights to talk, listen to music, and to just feel single. After a long marriage, it is a foreign experience to feel single. It took practice and courage for both of us to go to the bar together, having absolutely no intention of picking up guys as is a current practice today.

We needed to practice single life, practice talking to strangers, and practice dancing when neither of us had danced for years. One determined guy liked me and often asked me to dance. He kept asking me to go out to the car with him. "Absolutely not," I said. "You are married and should not be asking anyone to leave this setting."

One night, Kelly and I were sitting at a table when I saw my son and his girlfriend come into the bar. I hoped he wouldn't see me, and I thought about hiding out in the bathroom. But, I couldn't be so lucky. When he saw me with my friends, he said hi without coming over to our table. I spoke up too hastily, saying, "Doug, this is my new hangout now!" (What a stupid thing to call attention to this self he never knew!)

To be honest, he didn't think it was funny. "Oh, this is your hangout now," he said, mimicking what I said. That was the extent of the conversation before he left. Guilt oozed out every pore of my body, because he knew and I knew that Mom didn't hang out in bars. I told myself that I was a reformed person, and I shouldn't feel guilty for living my new life. Why did my old life shadow me everywhere I went? I needed to have the courage to say, "Get used to it, Susanne. You are not the same person anymore."

"Our kids don't know what we're going through," I said to Kelly. After their father died, they went on with their normal lives, and we don't have a normal life. "Besides, this third child of mine had his wild time through university life in a fraternity. And nothing I'd think of doing could compare to his life experiences."

The Dating Escapade

Kelly and I began to accept dinner invitations with different men we had met in the group. I had a friend, Harry, who was many years older than I was, and casual dinners helped time pass more quickly. I insisted on paying my own way with everyone I dated (until I met my future husband who wouldn't even consider letting me pick up the check). I wanted no expectations for payback. Harry answered questions about finances and other issues my husband had handled in my marriage. He was my confidant as well as a traveling partner. We planned several trips together, one to the Cayman Islands with my sister and her family.

Harry was the best male friend I could ever have, and I loved him dearly as a friend. He was such a fine person that it was hard not to consider him a candidate for marriage. I had made a firm resolution in my new reformed life that if I married, I wanted someone who would give me an unusual, maybe even unconventional, life than I have had before.

I made it very clear from the very beginning that marriage would not be part of this package. We were friends who could go out to movies, dinner, and widowed groups. With this arrangement, I felt I could go out with others, but this was unforgivable to him. After I accepted dates with someone else three different times, while trying to continue my friendship with Harry, the friendship ended.

Intimacy in Relationships

My wish for adventure and excitement remained an important goal for me. One night, I met a widowed man who wrote poetry. He had worked as a designer for a builder for many years. We began sending poems back and forth through e-mail, and we went out together a few times. Then one day, I received a package in the mail. Inside the package was a box with two flowers tied together with a ribbon: a daffodil and an Irish rose. He was Irish with a wonderful sense of humor, and he had written a poem to me and sent it with two beautiful flowers. You may get some idea of the content of his poem from the response I wrote to him called "The Drama in the Flower Bed."

    I know from my six years of experience in the Widowed Persons' Group that almost all men weren't willing to remain friends with one person very long without a sexual relationship. Every widowed woman I knew, except one, had the same experience. I knew one fine man who was dedicated to his partner. They went everywhere together, except he had to go home alone at 10:00 p m every night! The need for intimacy is understandable because many widowed people had a long struggle to care for their spouses before death. Some women wanted to delay that kind of intimacy, but others were as eager as men. To spend a considerable amount of time with most men, intimacy would be an expected part of the relationship.

    Eddie and I had never traveled. I grew up on a farm where no one ever went anywhere except to a different town. Every summer vacation after we moved to Virginia, Eddie and I with our family traveled to our hometown to keep in touch with their grandparents and cousins. Then, with Eddie's illness, vacation wasn't possible except for the last trip just a month before his death. Eddie died before he reached the age of retirement, which limited my income after his death, and I had been a stay-at-home-mother with my children when they were young, preventing me from retiring from teaching with full benefits. I would not be a wealthy widow.

SOUND OF MY SONG

The Drama in the Flower Bed

In the midst of beauty in a garden home
in the deep rich earth, once forest loam,
lives daffodils and hyacinths in shades of blue
and an Irish rose with a yellow hue.
"Daffodil," said Rose in a quiet tone.
"Sway with me in our garden home.

Sweet Daffodil, with your yellow shade,
waving gently on a green stem blade,
come close to me in our garden bed."
Daffodil blushed a pale shade of red.
Her petals quivered in the gentle breeze,
hearing the whispers of willow trees.

"I don't know what I want," said Daffodil.
"But, then again, maybe tomorrow I will.
Here where I am *now* is where I belong,
safely secured when the wind blows strong,
Not part of a spray in a kitchen bright,
nor on a fresh grave in the dead of night,
Not in your bed where you want me to be,
but instead *unconfined* in the garden, free.

I'm released as of now from my bittersweet past,
and cast in the daffodil drama at last,
gathering with others in the garden scene,
creating a fugue with the fairy queen.
You can join, too, with your keen Irish wit.
Indeed, an experience you'll never forget.
Stay loose, Irish Rose, with a life that's freestyle,
and join in the fun unrestrained for a while.

Forget at this time that winter looms near,
and the garden is cold when the snow blows here.
Forget, if you can, your poignant past,
and join in some free-flowing fun unsurpassed.
Then later, midst the beauty of our garden home
in the deep, rich earth, once forest loam,
you may find a daffodil or a hyacinth blue,
delighted to share a warm bed space with you."

For the Love of Lyrics

Today I am different from yesterday.
I read a book, I saw a sunset,
and I met you.
Images from your esoteric verse
flow through my mind
as I fall asleep.
Your thoughts run deep
like the rivers and seas
you elucidate.

In lyrical lines,
we open our lives to another
baring the soul,
tapping the longing within us,
trying to fill the deepest well
left empty by our loss,
searching
for the passage
to intimacy.

Because we have experienced
the death of a love,
we know the fragility of life.
Death teaches us
to appreciate
the significance of each day,
yearning for new meaning
to our existence.

KARMEN WORDEN

Today is unexplored,
but I savor the beauty in words
and ideas and the individuality
and creativity
that we each express
and extend
to one another,
exploring the possibility
of a new life
tomorrow.

I Wondered

I used to wonder when I was young
How people live each day,
When they are old, and the
End may be near.
Do they approach each day in fear?
Now I'm old and this I know,
Each day adds wonder to my soul.
I want another day to live.
I still have more of life to give.
I won't think about the past,
Or anticipate the future.
I live today without a sorrow
That I may not be here
Tomorrow.

Heaven

I think I'd like to mention
That I think of heaven
As a sixth dimension.
It can't be part of our Milky Way
Or near to the moon or a star.
It can't be anywhere in outer space
For God to be that far?
Let's imagine that heaven may be
Here, not visible for us to see
But somewhere close,
Where all is well,
The special place
Where God does
Dwell.

The hospice also announced that they have trained individual counselors who can be assigned to you-—mainly someone to talk with by phone. One day, I received the call from the woman named Peg, who said she had been asked to be a partner, and if I wanted, we could meet in a coffee shop. I met with Peg and loved her from the moment we met. I knew that Peg would be there to help me when I needed her. Nights were always the worst time of day, and thankfully, Peg had always been a night person, a habit from a life of nursing during evening hours. I could call her at 11:00 p.m. and midnight, and she was always willing to listen.

I tried to go to church, sitting near the back, and when the choir stood to sing their beautiful, opening song for the service, I'd think, "Will I make it through the service for once?" Most of the times in the first months, I rushed out during the first song. Once, the minister caught me and said, "Do you want to talk in the office?" I shook my head no, and at the same time, smeared his beautiful, white stole with my makeup.

The Child and the Wild

My premise is this: to make a marriage work, we sometimes have to give up parts of ourselves that have made us truly "who we are." We adapt our lives to live in peace in our relationships, and sometimes it is the child who withdraws. The characteristics of the child may not be accepted by a partner and can easily be squelched.

Dr. Harris said in his book "I'm Okay! You're Okay," "In the Child resides creativity, curiosity, the desire to explore and know, the urges to touch and feel the experience." I'm aware that it is an ancient book, but this part of the book fits the need for widowed people to find their child. Also, Dr. Harris said that the expressions of teasing, delight, laughter, and the joy of having fun—all stem from the child in all of us. Allowing these positive characteristics of a child to emerge can help a person move on in a new relationship which is strange, scary, and unfamiliar.

Jake, My Mistake

I never expected that I would meet someone like Jake, a fun-loving guy who had a cute way of walking, rather like a four-year-old all full of himself, and his shoulders having their own motions as he walked. I knew he wasn't anything like me nor would he like the typical kinds of things I would like to do. He was different, a "free spirit," and I had never known any male who fit that description. We began to go out for meals, as well as attending widowed activities together.

He fit my image of meeting people whom I would never have known in my former life, and he wouldn't fit the kind of life I would want in the future. His boyish personality fit my need to become aware of the wild child who wanted to play before I met someone to marry. No one I met had, in any way, been congruous with my objectives: a different kind of life than my past and someone intelligent and adventurous. Jake didn't excel in intelligence at this stage of his life, but he had an adventurous spirit. But I learned that his spirit was aided by the alcohol he drank daily.

Never had I ever met up with someone completely different who needed alcohol during the day. I had never let "wild child" loose, and to be honest, she didn't know how to be wild. Simply going out with this kind of guy was wild enough. I was naive not to realize that Jake was an alcoholic. I told him he was losing brain cells for every swallow of alcohol he took, although it was too late to change the habits of a lifetime. I had only been around people who didn't drink alcoholic beverages.

I had never been out with anyone who needed two martinis for lunch, while I never had more than two glasses of wine for an evening meal if we went to a restaurant. One noon, I tried one-half of a martini that frizzled my equilibrium for an hour. His body was acclimated to alcohol, and foolishly, I never felt he wasn't a safe driver. We'd go to one bar where people would drink, eat peanuts, and throw the shucks on the floor. Who lived this kind of life? Never anyone I had ever known.

One weekend when my daughter and her family came home, I invited Jake to dinner. We were sitting around the table with an empty seat for Jake when I decided to call him to see where he was. "I'm mowing the lawn," he said. "Do I have time to finish it before I come?"

I yelled at him, "No, and you are no longer welcome to come." It was an embarrassing moment as my daughter, who was religious and conservative, wouldn't consider I'd go out with anyone who didn't have basic manners of being on time when they were an invited guest.

For New Year's Eve, we planned a night at a hotel where we would dine, dance, and enjoy the typical celebration of the New Year. We had fun dancing when I decided to go back to my room for a few minutes. When I returned, wild guy and wild woman were in a frenzied dance, both of them whirling, spinning, and gyrating around like the primitive campfire in my poem.

The Truth of the Story

I wanted to end the story as if New Year's Eve was a movie and that's how it should have ended. Now, I have to admit the truth. When I came back to the dance floor, I was furious with him for picking up someone else with such speed. My dream of the passionate dance around a campfire was just a dream, and I immediately went back to the room. Soon, he came to the room and talked me into returning to the dance floor. As far as the "runaway release of passion in the night," here is another truth: Alcohol withers away more than just the brain. After I ended my relationship with Jake, I learned that he had been kicked out of the widowed group, because he had pinched two women on their butts. He had to exit the group in disgrace. That still makes me giggle.

In Jake's defense, he had been married to a European woman and had two intelligent, well-adjusted children. He had been faithful to his wife, although he had told me about a wild life before he met her. Maybe this was his only chance to return to his previous nature and enjoy reliving his earlier life one last time with me.

One night after a widowed group potluck, Kelly and I went to the bar with Michael and Bill, two guys from the widowed group. Of course, I didn't know at this time that Michael was interested in me. While we were drinking wine and talking, Jake came in to say hello at our table, took out a key, and said to me "Do you want your key back?" like he had a key to my house. It was a car key as he had once taken my car to a service station. I was quite embarrassed as Michael was at the table with me, Kelly, and Bill.

I remember telling friends in the support group about meeting a guy from the Internet. Michael was in the widowed support group at that time, the man who would eventually be my husband who you met at the beginning of the story when we drove down the lane to my humble farm. Later, Michael said, "Remember, when you talked about meeting someone on the Internet and you told the group about it?" Of course, I remembered that. He said, "I thought at the time. Why is she doing that when she has me?"

Of course, he was fairly new to the group and why would he think I had him. He was a Jew whom I would never consider dating, anyway. We had never dated. If I had known that he thought he had me, I would have thought, "What kind of arrogance is that?"

Then, I remembered my prayer for the open door. This fits with the person whom I would find who wouldn't necessarily fit my ideas of someone I'd want to marry. Truly, is God guiding me to be with my personal Jew? How could this be possible? I thought God knew my thoughts and my needs for another life. Maybe He did and I did not know myself.

Truly, this was the open door as I had not encouraged Michael. He remembered my name in the potluck evening. He came to the support group I facilitated. He has asked me to go out with him three times. Now, he's asking me why I'd go to the Internet to find someone who would fit my ideas of a second husband when I had him! Also, I once asked members in the support group what characteristic or traits would be necessary for a future mate. After many people had shared their ideas, I remember saying, "For me, spirituality is important. A partner would have to have a spiritual connection."

Michael rarely talked in the group, but he asked me directly, "What do you mean by spiritual?" I hesitated for a while before I answered, "Christianity." In later years, I reminded him of this dialogue and asked why, since he was Jewish, that didn't discourage his interest in me.

He said, "I considered it a challenge." I'm moving ahead in the story just to relate that there was spiritual energy breathing new life into a possible future attachment without my knowing it was there.

Kelly looked at me and we couldn't believe that Jake would bring me a key that belonged to me and in public, in front of a group, and in front of two men, one who would later become my husband. Jake lacked common, decent social skills or he wanted the guys to be reminded that I had once been connected to his life. He even had a key, they might think, to my house.

Later, I learned that others in the widowed group wondered why a person like me would date a man like Jake. After I found Michael, my new-husband-to-be, Ann said to me, "Finally, you found someone who was worthy of you." One night, I invited all couples who had been dating to my home where we had agreed to discuss our ideas of what to do about money in a second marriage. Ella was a part of our widowed group as were others like her who let men think that there are these kinds of women in support groups, too. Ella was there with the friend she was meeting.

Ella

Ella dresses hot
when she comes to our
group dinners
planned for people like us
now living alone.
Our loved ones
have died, and
we need to be with
people like us
who want to delay
going home
to an empty house.

We notice Ella because
she stands out, her
sexiness displayed
like fringes on a scarf.
The thickness of her
makeup, a cover for
the wrinkles,
but we know,
it covers a pretty face.

We see her with Jack
and wonder why
a respectable man like him
would go with her.
He could find
a woman
more worthy of him,
but we don't need
to ask.

KARMEN WORDEN

One night, I wore
a new black fuzzy scarf
which was in style.
Ella came to talk
to me.
She said she wanted
to wear her scarf, too,
just like mine,
but she didn't
want to look
like a hussy.

One day, we heard
a new man in the group
tell his story,
and we all know how
stories like this
pass on in the blink
of an eye.
He said he found
a panty in his pocket.
All of the women
willing to start over again
would want this guy,
who's really cool,
but Ella wanted
to get there first.

He knew, and
all of us knew,
that Ella
put it there.

SOUND OF MY SONG

One night at
a small party at my house,
we talked about money
and who should pay
the second time
around.

Are the rules different
than they were before?
Maybe, we both
have money
from the other life
and bills should be shared.
But Ella made it clear
after several drinks
that night,
and we laughed
when she said
with certainty,
"No money,
no honey."

Camels and Cornfields

I introduced Michael, my husband, at the beginning of the story when we drove down the lane to my rundown farm and my discomfort for him to see my humble beginnings. I also learned later that there seemed to be a spiritual energy emerging from Michael, breathing new life into a possible future attachment to me without my knowing it was there. Why, in support group when I shared my Internet dating experience, did he think to himself, "Why is she doing that, when she has me?" We had had no contact with each other besides the support group up to that time.

His interest began in a potluck group at a friend's home. Discovering this widowed group was like finding an illuminated cabin with smoke coming out of the chimney when you were lost in a forest. Those of us who had been in the group for a few years were particularly sensitive to the difficulties of first-time visitors, trying to help them feel welcome. We were there for the very same reason.

We all wore name tags, and I sat down on the ottoman in front of Michael's chair to introduce myself and ask him when he was widowed and if this was the first time he had come to a dinner. We visited for a short time, and I learned that he had grown up in Israel and had come to the States after his years in the Israeli army. I left to talk to someone else and never saw him again until he walked into my support group the next time we met.

The support group met in a cozy room in a church nearby, and Michael came dressed in a stylish suit, obviously coming directly from work. I thought he had a European aura about him, and he was different from anyone who'd ever visited our group. Michael shared some details about losing his wife to breast cancer, but most of the time he remained silent and listened to the discussion. I didn't know if he would ever return to the group, as some widowed people need to share their pain while others are uncomfortable talking about it with others. He seemed more comfortable listening to others. Truthfully, I thought he didn't look like the type of guy who would choose to come to a support group.

It was several meetings later when Michael asked me to go to the Kennedy Center to a pop concert of the symphony orchestra, and I agreed to go. I called Jenna my sister, saying, "It's safe to go out with this guy once because he's Jewish." We both knew what that meant. Since I was a faithful Christian and active in my church, I would never consider marrying outside of the faith.

My home town was a Protestant community: no Catholics, no Jews, and few people from a different culture walked into our town. We were isolated from the world, and we didn't even know it. I thought it would be fun to visit with someone who had lived a completely different life. I had no experience traveling during my lifetime. Farmers never traveled as they couldn't leave the animals, and time always limited their activities. Before Eddie's illness, travel plans gave me a hope for seeing countries of the world when the children had graduated from their universities. But my husband's illness limited all of our plans. My background coming to Israel was teaching in the county school many years after we moved to Virginia.

I had always had a fascination with Israel. To me, it was a place I never dreamed of visiting. We had fun that evening and each shared some of our life's experiences. I learned more details about his background. He had been working in New York after graduating from an engineering university there until he was asked to be in charge of expanding their engineering company office in Washington, DC. It was an interesting evening as we had come from such different worlds. I wondered if he would want to see me again.

Surprisingly, Michael came regularly to the support group, and when he asked me again to go to the Kennedy Center, then that was a different thing. I had second thoughts. I don't want to lead this guy on when he's someone who couldn't be part of my future. I turned him down and suggested my friend Kelly, who might enjoy the concert as Michael had season tickets.

When Kelly said she was busy, I said, "Let me go home and check my 'black book' to see what I have scheduled this week." I knew I didn't have anything scheduled, and he was sure I was putting him off until I called him that evening and told him I was free that night. I rarely had a chance to go to the Kennedy Center. We continued to see each other for dinners out and for concerts and plays.

Stories about Michael's Life

One night while sharing childhood memories, Michael said, "I remember camel caravans coming through the town from Jaffa, heading for the Yarkon River area, a river that dumps into the Mediterranean Sea. Arabs riding on donkeys led camels on their way to collect ziv-ziv (his term for sand mixed with grains of seashells which can be harvested and mixed with cement for building material in Jaffa)." I knew about Jaffa from my Bible studies, an ancient city next to Tel Aviv on the Mediterranean coast of Israel where Biblical Jonah supposedly set sail. Jaffa was also where St. Peter was thought to receive his divine instruction to preach to non-Jews.

Colorful pictures entered my mind—the visual imagery of camels and city life—so unfamiliar to me. My story seemed so humble and insignificant, as I told him about farm life, gravel roads, and raising animals for food. Camels in the desert were intriguing, and suddenly, I realized that the excitement of adventure loomed before me.

Other differences surfaced when we talked about his childhood. He lived in an apartment on a narrow street in the city, Tel Aviv, Israel. He explained, "My father started a bakery after he moved to Israel from Lithuania before Israel became a country in 1948. You wondered why I wouldn't want to spend a week near the Mediterranean Sea for a vacation? I grew up there. And for eighteen years, my friends and I ran to the beach after school." He said he lived in walking distance from orange groves, which were the main crops in Israel at that time.

Michael told me an interesting fact that could never happen in my farm setting. His father kept a gun under his mattress, the safest place for it to be. Who would look under a child's mattress for a weapon? During this time Great Britain, the United Kingdom, controlled Israel, and it was against the law for Israelis to join the underground groups for training when later they wanted to fight for their independence. Michael's father belonged to one underground unit. Also, he wanted the gun if protection would ever be needed from the Arab community who lived nearby.

"We" Became "Us"

I believe it was the third date when Michael started talking about us as if we were a couple. How "we" became an "us" to him, I'll never know. Yes, I thought I knew about the prayer, but the Great Creator who knew me could never select me to marry a Jewish man. Michael never asked me to marry him. But after the third night at the Kennedy Center, he drove me by to see his office in the city and back to see his house before he brought me home. When we visited by the fireplace in the evening, he even mentioned something about what he would leave for me after he died, although I did not understand what he meant and I did not take his words seriously. These latest talks about us were simply too new for me to understand and accept.

The problem was this: the next weekend, I was going for a weekend at the beach with Jake. He and I were in the process of ending the relationship, but I had promised to help him with the water damage from a recent storm in his apartment at the beach. While at the beach house one night, I went in another room and called Michael. He was so happy to hear from me, his voice quite sensual, saying that he missed me. He had kissed me only once the night we went back to his house. These are just the facts. I can't understand it myself.

Michael's Side of the Story

When I got home, I heard the whole story of how this all began. It started the first night I saw him at the potluck dinner when I sat down on the ottoman to talk to him for a few moments.

He saw the unusual spelling of my name and said he came to the support group because the newsletter said that I was the facilitator of the group. He told me about the Sunday I was gone to the beach and he didn't know where I was and how he kept calling my house all day. He said he had paced around the house, trying to call me repeatedly.

Knowing him as I do now, this was not typical behavior. He's not the "support group type of man." A week ago in present time, I asked him (for the fun of asking) that if we needed marriage counseling, "Would you go?"

"Of course not," he said. "But both of us know we would never need counseling.

I answered, "You went to the support group when you met me."

"That was different," he said.

I do have a sense of people's personalities from the support group that I had been facilitating for over five years, and he had been attending the group for several weeks. I contend that I have an intuitive sense when it comes to people. I remember one night in a potluck dinner group when I sat by a man who talked to me for an hour, he said, "I told you more about my life tonight than I've told anyone in my lifetime.

My Acceptance of Marriage

Some time ago when I had started to date, I talked to my friend JoAnn, who has a counseling degree and a writer, about the people I had met and how none of them came close to being the right person for me, "I was in my fifties, and I thought I was too young to live the rest of my life alone."

Her answer was this, "Ask God for help. Then wait for the open door." To me, this meant that if I never met anyone suitable for marriage, then it was meant to be. I wouldn't make any effort but to just let it happen. Prayer has always been a part of my life, just in my thoughts as I go through the day. I am thankful that I can pray directly to God at any time of the day and ask for forgiveness for times I have not done the right thing. Then, when I met Michael and suddenly I was the right person for him, what would you think?

My son-in-law said, "I don't believe in such things." He didn't think that God enters into the decision of whom we marry, and maybe he's right. I know I am married only because I thought this unusual development was the *open door*; that it was meant to be.

I called my sister to tell her I was getting married, and she was shocked. I got a lecture about making a decision too fast, and I hung up on my best friend. I was upset with her for several months because she should have congratulated me on my upcoming marriage.

I called my daughter, and she told me I always had the tendency to be impulsive! Since when had I been impulsive? Did that mean that every time I told her something I planned to do and changed my mind, I had been impulsive—to even think of the original idea?

Kelly and I talked about people in the group who had problems with their children interfering with a mother's or father's relationship. Children have no right to tell their parents how to live their lives. My children's father died, but they still had normal lives with their families. I, as a widowed mother, had my normal life broken into pieces.

I called my youngest son, and he said over and over, "I'm shocked. I'm shocked." None of my children had ever heard Michael's name. This decision happened before I had a chance to talk to the children. I felt just as shocked as my children by the unconventional commitment I had made. I visualized my mother asking for a counseling session with God, saying, "See what my daughter did now? She's marrying a Jew. What can You do about that?"

My second son was happy. I didn't know he had promised his Japanese wife that they'd live some years of their married life in Japan. After his dad died, how could he leave his mother here alone? (He is that kind of child.) After I told him about the marriage, he said that they could now plan to look for a job in Japan. He knew that someone was here to take care of me. The thought brings tears in my eyes—just that he waited until he knew I would have a new life with someone watching over me.

We told Michael's children too early about coming for an engagement party which was six months after Michael's wife died. They were upset and wouldn't come, and we cancelled the party. They were still mad about our marriage at the wedding six months later. Michael's son-in-law asked my daughter, "Are you as unhappy about this marriage as we are?" I was proud that she answered, "I trust my mother to make the right decisions." (I guess she had forgotten that she thought I was impulsive or wouldn't admit it to my in-laws.)

Thankfully, it wasn't too long before I developed a good relationship with his children, but it didn't happen overnight. I kept telling his children that Michael had not forgotten their mother. He put flowers on her grave, and on the anniversary of her death, he burned a candle on the day of her death, which was traditional for him, even for his parents.

One time when Michael's grandson was eating lunch at our home, he said, "I remember buying that salt and pepper shaker set for my grandma." I sent it home with him the same day. Soon, I was taking Michael's two grandchildren bowling and for miniature golf, and helping the younger son with his homework. One of the happiest moments in my life came a few years ago when his daughter sent me flowers on Mother's Day, a beautiful gesture I never expected, and she has sent the flowers every year since that day.

The Wedding

We planned a beautiful Jewish/Christian wedding in a very upscale restaurant in Washington, DC. We followed some Jewish traditions—the canopy (Chuppah), a symbol of the new home the bride and groom will share as husband and wife. At the end of the service, he stepped on a glass to break it. The reason for this tradition unknown. Originally, it may have meant that despite the joy, Jews still mourn the destruction of the Temple in Jerusalem. For Michael who was a secular Jew, it was simply a tradition. We hired a dance band and a violin played during part of the service. We walked in together, and had no one sing and no one stand up with us. The service included only Michael and me.

    This rabbi performs mixed marriages and has a service he uses taken from the book of Ruth. My minister was happy to be a part of it. The beautiful words lay right next to my heart. Ruth 1:16 says, "Whither thou goest, I will go; and where thou lodgest, I will lodge; thy people shall be my people, and thy God my God." Some friends in the widowed group told me it was one of the most beautiful weddings they had seen.

Our First Trip to Israel

I could hardly contain my excitement as we planned our first trip to Israel together. Michael hired a guide to take us to all the Christian sites, as well as other places of importance to Jews. Of course, he knew his country well, but he couldn't have explained the Christian sites to me. I had read the guides about going to Israel, and one issue surprised me: the Jerusalem Syndrome.

This condition happens to some people who are so overcome being near the home of Jesus that these symptoms arouse this kind of passion: some have psychotic ideas, some symptoms come from religious convictions, and the third group includes sane people without psychiatric history without drugs and arrive as normal tourists with these conditions. Sometimes, the syndrome is severe enough to require a stay in the hospital. I envisioned my embarrassment if I would begin to babble and my hair stood on end as I visited sacred Christian sites with my Jewish relatives seeing me so overcome by the emotions of being in the Holy Land.

Truthfully, I had a different view about seeing these holy places in the middle of beautiful churches with stained glass windows, the look of gold everywhere, and all exquisite sites adorned like the decoration done by the Greek Orthodox Churches. I didn't think that Jesus or John the Baptist would be comfortable in the churches dedicated to them. I wanted to see John the Baptist's cave. I wanted to see the places like they were pictured in my mind, not in the middle of such spectacular beauty. Jesus sat among the ordinary people, the poor, the crippled, and the fishermen, and he had plenty of criticism about the Pharisees.

But I do understand our human need to create beautiful churches to honor Jesus and others who lived during the time of Jesus. On a later trip, I asked to see John the Baptist's cave and Michael's sister drove down some curvy, narrow gravel roads to get there only to see a sign saying that there were special hours when you could enter the cave with a guide. We could see the opening of the cave through a fence.

Feeling the Site of the Cross

To touch the hole in the rock where Jesus hung on the cross, I had to crouch on my knees under a table and put my hand down in a hole to feel the rock and the indented section where the cross had stood. It seemed unreal. I know that the wife of Constantine during the AD 300 felt it was necessary to find the exact sites where these events took place. It doesn't matter that there are disagreements about whether all of these sites are accurately placed since I am in this beautiful land, and the events that happened are close by. I wondered if the act of kneeling on the floor to feel where the cross had stood was purposely planned to be an act of humility as we experienced the sacredness of the site of the cross.

We walked the Via Dolorosa, the fourteen stations of the cross where we followed people who would kneel down and kiss the stone path. A few places had a sign saying it may have been the original stone floor. We visited the Church of the Nativity, which is an Arab city where our Jewish guide wouldn't drive us near to the church. He parked outside in a safe location, and we took a taxi driven by an Arab to the church. There in the basement of the Church of the Nativity, we saw the place where Jesus was born. It is wonderful to be in the land that we've heard so much about in the Bible, but since I did not expect that it was necessarily the exact location of His birth, I think I was safe from experiencing the Jerusalem syndrome.

In the past, our Jewish guide's car had been stoned by Arabs as he drove close to the Church of the Nativity. His insurance had become too high for him to continue his job as a guide in Arab territory. When we came out of the church and the bus loads of tourists were gone, Michael looked around only to see Arabs selling souvenir items, and in discomfort he said, "Let's leave here right away." We rushed to the exit.

Even in Michael's own country, these are the Arab cities where he would feel unwelcome, although our first trip to Israel came before the Second Intifada when fighting between Palestinians and Jews continued again. It started after Ariel Sharon went into the Temple Mount, a sacred place to the Muslims where Mohammed was believed to have ascended into heaven. They say that the footprint of his horse is embedded in the rock. Also, it is thought to be the place where Abraham took Isaac to be sacrificed. Yet, Jews are not allowed in the Temple Mount because it now belongs to the Arabs. To the Jews, it is a sacred site where the Second Temple of Solomon stood.

The only block wall standing where the Second Temple originally was located, the "Wailing Wall" continues to be a sacred place for the Jews. There, Jews go to pray and place notes to God in cracks in the wall. Orthodox Jews in their black suits, hats, long hair, and beards stand or sit in the position of movement, forward and back, forward and back, as they pray in the presence of the Sacred Wall.

In the marketplace in Jerusalem, the guide said "Get behind me", and he told Michael to follow after me, as people, he said, have been killed in this marketplace. Understand that we were alone, not with a group of tourists on a bus. Traveling with a tour group, you would be in safe surroundings to visit the country. Michael knows where to go, but for this visit, they were taking me places they wouldn't ordinarily visit. Most people can recognize Jews when they see them, and there are places in Israel as well as other countries where Michael would not be welcome to travel.

Every trip to Israel has been a highlight of my life. Michael's sister, who lives there, has gone out of her way to take me places where I would like to go. I wanted to see Cana where Jesus performed his first miracle, which is another Arab city. We visited the church which was built over the original site of the synagogue that Jesus visited. We took the stairs down to the excavated section underneath the building, allowing visitors to view a part of the original synagogue as it was in Jesus' day. Along one wall, we saw huge jars made of pottery that held water or wine.

One other highlight from our trips was the Garden of Gethsemane where Jesus prayed with His disciples. In an area surrounded by a fence, the same old Olive trees stood there like soldiers marking the sacred place. Since these trees were thought to be the same trees in the time of Jesus, I could imagine Jesus there praying with his disciples before his crucifixion

On another visit, I wanted to go up the mountain where the Transfiguration took place, since that site was the sermon that changed my views of Christianity. Michael's sister drove us around and around Mount Tabor, where on the summit, a church and one or two monasteries are located. There, a mural presents the story of Jesus with the three disciples and Moses and Elijah. We enjoyed the beautiful setting on Mount Tabor as we viewed the land of Israel in the valley below. Others think that the Transfiguration happened on a different mountain, but one has to believe the accepted view.

Traveling to archaeological sites has been a favorite part of our trips. After watching one documentary on television showing an excavated Roman City called Tzippori, also known as Sapphires just five kilometers from Nazareth, we had to visit this impressive site with a Roman theatre, a synagogue, and floors decorated with beautiful mosaic stones. The documentary reported that the site during the time of Jesus would have been a bustling city of wealthy Romans, and they speculated that it would have been possible for Joseph and Jesus to have worked there during the time of Jesus. This also would have placed Jesus in a location where contact with the Romans would have been expected.

Country in a Kibbutz

Masada was built on top of a flat mountain 1,000 ft. above the Dead Sea. It was built as a palace for Herod as a place of safety for him, with storehouses for foods, bathhouses, and even servant's quarters. It was excavated in 1963, and a cable car takes visitors to the top of the mountain where tour guides explain the story of Masada. They point out the place on the desert floor where you can see the site where Roman soldiers camped until they could build a ramp around the mountain to the top to kill the remaining Jews, the last of the Jewish resistance.

The story tells that the Jews on the mountain committed suicide rather than be taken by the Romans. Thus, it is a well-known popular tourist site. Since it is a very important place to Jews, I was shocked when our guide began shouting at an Arab guide. I couldn't understand the language, but Michael said he was offended that an Arab guide didn't have the proper license to take tourists to such a reverent place that represented an emotional saga in Jewish history.

Another interesting moment happened when we drove into the Kibbutz, and the guide explained that the tank that was left at the entrance was a Syrian tank. Ike, who grew up in Israel, knew differently. He said, "No, it is an Iraqi tank." The guide was shocked. He wasn't born in Israel but came there like many others after it became a homeland for the Jews in 1948. He said, "For forty years, I have been telling visitors that it was a Syrian tank." He learned something new that very day.

One incident happened where I caused Michael embarrassment. The guide drove into a Kibbutz just to show me the communities that had been established after Israel became a country in 1948. This one was Kibbutz Genosar, all of them rural communities set up years ago to reclaim the soil of the ancient homeland and to forge a new way of life. They were socialist communities based on joint ownership of the property. Many of these kibbutzim are not used for agriculture today. Each one may have a different product to sell, like one may be for diamonds.

The buildings included members' homes and gardens, children's houses, playgrounds, a swimming pool, and medical clinic just to name a few of the buildings which allowed the members to be completely self-sufficient. Next to the living quarters were sheds for dairy cattle, chicken coops, and other buildings to suit their needs. As we drove into the kibbutz, the guide circled around the cow shed, and suddenly I said, "Stop the car. I want to take a picture of the cows." This was still a new marriage and Michael had never been angry with me.

"You want us to stop the car to take a picture of the cows in Israel?" Michael yelled.

I stammered, saying that because my brother was a farmer, I wanted to show him a different kind of farming community. Michael sat there not moving until the guide said, "Give in on the small things and save the anger for more important issues." Then Michael got out of the car, angrily took a picture of the cows, got in the car, and slammed the door. I sat in the backseat having problems keeping tears at bay for the rest of the day. I think it may have been Michael's embarrassment revealing his wife's country background to a Jewish guide that caused his outburst. I guess I will never know when the country in me escapes and enters my present life, causing shock when I suddenly realize what I have done. Whoever went to the holy land and took a picture of a cow? It was only later years that I understood what an insult it was to Michael to stop the car and take that picture. It took some time in my marriage to learn that Michael is truly a "renaissance man." A renaissance person is one who is skilled in multiple fields or multiple disciplines who knows several languages and who has a broad base of knowledge. Michael knows classical music and composers, humming along with the music, knowing the phrases that will come next. He knows most of the classical operas, as well as the name of literary classics and their authors. He has amazing knowledge of history and a good memory of important events and dates. However, no one would know this unless they knew him as well as I do. He is quiet about his past, never letting anyone know in casual conversations that he has this kind of knowledge.

Ike's parents spoke Yiddish, Polish, Lithuanian, Russian, as well as Hebrew because they grew up in the area of Lithuania that was sometimes ruled by Russia, Poland, or Lithuania. Michael learned Arabic and English in high school. He knew German because a German family in an apartment below them never learned Hebrew. In addition, German has similarities to Yiddish. He knows enough Spanish to understand and communicate because his first wife was Spanish.

I asked Michael if his sister's children have the same background as he did in the classics. "Not at all," he said. Today, they can travel anywhere in Europe. They can expand their minds in their travels. They don't need to read it in books.

Interesting reasons exist for Michael's generation to have this kind of knowledge. During those years when Michael was growing up, war surrounded Israel and all around Europe. They could not travel. They could only expand their minds. They had the radio, Michael said, which broadcast music from all over Europe. They knew Italian musicians and French singers and classical and popular music. Music, opera, or classics from Germany were against the law. One high school friend who came from a wealthy family had a hi-fi and they would go to his house after school to listen to these recordings, happy to have a friend with such luxury. Imagine our high school students in the U.S. leaving high school in the afternoon to listen to classics at a friend's home.

Maybe my daughter was right when she said, "Mom, you sometimes do impulsive things." I never thought that was true. Asking Michael to take a picture of a cow in Israel is about the most outrageous, impulsive act I can ever imagine. This time, dear daughter, only this time you are absolutely right.

This time, Mom made an appointment with the Creator, and she said. "Dear God, do you see what my daughter did now? She's marrying a Jew."

The Creator said, "Margaret, she's following her own inner Spirit. Just let her go."

KARMEN WORDEN

Change of Pace

I want to take a meditative break
from reality and deliberation
and everything that requires
any serious concentration,
from left-brain control of meticulosity
to right brain wholeness
A restful state of unity.
I want the luxury of dreaming,
time to ponder and explore,
to reflect on a thought
or create a metaphor.
I want an attitude of wonder
like the innocence of a child,
the intrigue of fascination,
some thoughts that border wild.
I want to ponder, to commune,
a spiritual contemplation,
a time for musing on the mystical,
time for imagination
and
Celebration!

The Second Time Around

"How is life
the second time around?"
they ask?
"We've learned what not to do," I say.
"Life is peaceful every day.
When you know each day
could be your last,
the days of silent times have passed.
We've learned to let it go, move on,
not caring if we've lost or won.
We know it isn't worth the pain
to rehash words
with nothing to gain.

Sometimes I'm sorry
for something I said.
He says to me,
"What was it you did?"
He doesn't remember,
The moment had passed.
It's such a relief,
such freedom at last.
To be fair, we must think
we have limited tension
in a second-time marriage
and living on pension.

There is no doubt.
Indeed there's no mystery,
that we've left our past lives,
and we won't repeat history.
We wake up each morning
to enjoy the day's light,
and we're joyful to tell you,
we sleep well at night."

Questions for Discussion

Susanne felt she must have been dropped into a wrong family. Have any of you ever felt that way? Why or why not?

What were your opinions about depression before you read the story?

Did your opinions change after reading the story? How? Why? Why not?

Is it more difficult to suppress something that happened to you - or - share it to a friend or in a group. Can sharing it cause a lifting of pressure, or even freedom, or maybe the possibility of a new friendship

Or were you bothered later that you had shared? Do you know why?

What might keep people from accepting depression, no different than diabetics needing insulin?

Did you understand why the sermon on Transfiguration changed Susanne in the story?

Can you think of something you have read or learned that has changed your life in some way - or changed your mind?

Did one character make a choice that had more implications, would you have made the same decision? Explain.

About the Author

Karmen left the farm for a mid-western university, studying music and education. She taught upper-grade children for twenty-three years in Iowa and Virginia. She married her high school sweetheart, and after he graduated from Iowa State University with a PhD in economics, they moved to Virginia.

As a teacher, she wrote plays and musicals to enrich her students' lives. When they studied "early man" she wrote "The Cave Man Rap," which was performed for two consecutive years for students in school and for parents in the evening. Her love for music led her to writing songs for her students' plays about settlers moving west. Teacher Magazine published her article "Puppets, a Key to Music" after the study of the westward movement sparked interest in puppet plays.

During the same time period, she wrote the book *The Lives of John the Baptist and Peter,* which was used with the new Sunday school curriculum in her church published by Augsburg Publishing Company. In addition, she wrote three family histories telling the story of her ancestors—the Swedish and Norwegian families. The last German history was for her husband who died before his youngest child was married and to leave a legacy for the grandchildren who would never know the love he would have for them. The Sound of My Song, Susanne Stephenson's story, was written by Karmen Worden.

CPSIA information can be obtained
at www.ICGtesting.com
Printed in the USA
FFOW03n1415010717
37256FF